Flash CS3: Basic

Instructor's Edition

Flash CS3: Basic

President & Chief Executive Officer:	Michael Springer
Vice President, Product Development:	Adam A. Wilcox
Vice President, Operations:	Josh Pincus
Director of Publishing Systems Development:	Dan Quackenbush
Developmental Editor:	Micky Markert
Series Designer:	Adam A. Wilcox

Trademarks

Disclaimer

We reserve the right to revise this publication and make changes from time to time in its content without notice.

ISBN 10: 1-4260-9725-5
ISBN 13: 978-1-4260-9725-6

Printed in the United States of America

1 2 3 4 5 6 7 8 9 10 GL 10 09 08

Contents

Introduction

After reading this introduction, you will know how to:

A Use ILT Series manuals in general.

B Use prerequisites, a target student description, course objectives, and a skills inventory to properly set students' expectations for the course.

C Set up a classroom to teach this course.

D Get support for setting up and teaching this course.

Topic A: About the manual

ILT Series philosophy

Our goal is to make you, the instructor, as successful as possible. To that end, our manuals facilitate students' learning by providing structured interaction with the software itself. While we provide text to help you explain difficult concepts, the hands-on activities are the focus of our courses. Leading the students through these activities will teach the skills and concepts effectively.

We believe strongly in the instructor-led class. For many students, having a thinking, feeling instructor in front of them will always be the most comfortable way to learn. Because the students' focus should be on you, our manuals are designed and written to facilitate your interaction with the students, and not to call attention to manuals themselves.

We believe in the basic approach of setting expectations, then teaching, and providing summary and review afterwards. For this reason, lessons begin with objectives and end with summaries. We also provide overall course objectives and a course summary to provide both an introduction to and closure on the entire course.

Our goal is your success. We encourage your feedback in helping us to continually improve our manuals to meet your needs.

Manual components

The manuals contain these major components:

- Table of contents
- Introduction
- Units
- Appendix
- Course summary
- Quick reference
- Glossary
- Index

Each element is described below.

Table of contents

The table of contents acts as a learning roadmap for you and the students.

Introduction

The introduction contains information about our training philosophy and our manual components, features, and conventions. It contains target student, prerequisite, objective, and setup information for the specific course. Finally, the introduction contains support information.

Units

Units are the largest structural component of the actual course content. A unit begins with a title page that lists objectives for each major subdivision, or topic, within the unit. Within each topic, conceptual and explanatory information alternates with hands-on activities. Units conclude with a summary comprising one paragraph for each topic, and an independent practice activity that gives students an opportunity to practice the skills they've learned.

The conceptual information takes the form of text paragraphs, exhibits, lists, and tables. The activities are structured in two columns, one telling students what to do, the other providing explanations, descriptions, and graphics. Throughout a unit, instructor notes are found in the left margin.

Course summary

This section provides a text summary of the entire course. It is useful for providing closure at the end of the course. The course summary also indicates the next course in this series, if there is one, and lists additional resources students might find useful as they continue to learn about the software.

Quick reference

The quick reference is an at-a-glance job aid summarizing some of the more common features of the software.

Glossary

The glossary provides definitions for all of the key terms used in this course.

Index

The index at the end of this manual makes it easy for you and your students to find information about a particular software component, feature, or concept.

Manual conventions

We've tried to keep the number of elements and the types of formatting to a minimum in the manuals. We think this aids in clarity and makes the manuals more classically elegant looking. But there are some conventions and icons you should know about.

Item	Description
Italic text	In conceptual text, indicates a new term or feature.
Bold text	In unit summaries, indicates a key term or concept. In an independent practice activity, indicates an explicit item that you select, choose, or type.
`Code font`	Indicates code or syntax.

`Longer strings of ►`
`    code will look ►`
`    like this.`
	In the hands-on activities, any code that's too long to fit on a single line is divided into segments by one or more continuation characters (►). This code should be entered as a continuous string of text.

	In the left margin, provide tips, hints, and warnings for the instructor.
Select **bold item**	In the left column of hands-on activities, bold sans-serif text indicates an explicit item that you select, choose, or type.
Keycaps like ⏎ ENTER	Indicate a key on the keyboard you must press.
	Warnings prepare instructors for potential classroom management problems.
	Tips give extra information the instructor can share with students.
	Setup notes provide a realistic business context for instructors to share with students, or indicate additional setup steps required for the current activity.
	Projector notes indicate that there is a PowerPoint slide for the adjacent content.

Instructor notes.

⚠ *Warning icon.*

✔ *Tip icon.*

Setup icon.

Projector icon.

Hands-on activities

The hands-on activities are the most important parts of our manuals. They are divided into two primary columns. The "Here's how" column gives short directions to the students. The "Here's why" column provides explanations, graphics, and clarifications. To the left, instructor notes provide tips, warnings, setups, and other information for the instructor only. Here's a sample:

Do it!

A-1: Creating a commission formula

Here's how	Here's why
Take the time to make sure your students understand this worksheet. We'll be here a while.	
1 Open Sales	This is an oversimplified sales compensation worksheet. It shows sales totals, commissions, and incentives for five sales reps.
2 Observe the contents of cell F4	`F4  ▼    =  =E4*C_Rate`
	The commission rate formulas use the name "C_Rate" instead of a value for the commission rate.

For these activities, we have provided a collection of data files designed to help students learn each skill in a real-world business context. As students work through the activities, they will modify and update these files. Of course, students might make a mistake and therefore want to re-key the activity starting from scratch. To make it easy to start over, students will rename each data file at the end of the first activity in which the file is modified. Our convention for renaming files is to add the word "My" to the beginning of the file name. In the above activity, for example, students are using a file called "Sales" for the first time. At the end of this activity, they would save the file as "My sales," thus leaving the "Sales" file unchanged. If students make mistakes, they can start over using the original "Sales" file.

In some activities, however, it might not be practical to rename the data file. Such exceptions are indicated with an instructor note. If students want to retry one of these activities, you will need to provide a fresh copy of the original data file.

PowerPoint presentations

Each unit in this course has an accompanying PowerPoint presentation. These slide shows are designed to support your classroom instruction while providing students with a visual focus. Each presentation begins with a list of unit objectives and ends with a unit summary slide. We strongly recommend that you run these presentations from the instructor's station as you teach this course. A copy of PowerPoint Viewer is included, so it is not necessary to have PowerPoint installed on your computer.

The ILT Series PowerPoint add-in

The CD also contains a PowerPoint add-in that enables you to do two things:

- Create slide notes for the class
- Display a control panel for the Flash movies embedded in the presentations

To load the PowerPoint add-in:

1   Copy the Course_ILT.ppa file to a convenient location on your hard drive.
2   Start PowerPoint.
3   Choose Tools, Macro, Security to open the Security dialog box. On the Security Level tab, select Medium (if necessary), and then click OK.
4   Choose Tools, Add-Ins to open the Add-Ins dialog box. Then, click Add New.
5   Browse to and double-click the Course_ILT.ppa file, and then click OK. A message box will appear, warning you that macros can contain viruses.
6   Click Enable Macros. The Course_ILT add-in should now appear in the Available Add-Ins list (in the Add-Ins dialog box). The "x" in front of Course_ILT indicates that the add-in is loaded.
7   Click Close to close the Add-Ins dialog box.

After you complete this procedure, a new toolbar will be available at the top of the PowerPoint window. This toolbar contains a single button labeled "Create SlideNotes." Click this button to generate slide-notes files in both text (.txt) and Excel (.xls) format. By default, these files will be saved to the folder that contains the presentation. If the PowerPoint file is on a CD-ROM or in some other location to which the slide-notes files cannot be saved, you will be prompted to save the presentation to your hard drive and try again.

When you run a presentation and come to a slide that contains a Flash movie, you will see a small control panel in the lower-left corner of the screen. You can use this panel to start, stop, and rewind the movie, or to play it again.

Topic B: Setting student expectations

Properly setting students' expectations is essential to your success. This topic will help you do that by providing:

- Prerequisites for this course
- A description of the target student
- A list of the objectives for the course
- A skills assessment for the course

Course prerequisites

Students taking this course should be familiar with personal computers and the use of a keyboard and a mouse. Furthermore, this course assumes that students have completed the following courses or have equivalent experience:

- *Windows XP: Basic* or *Windows Vista: Basic*

Target student

Students taking this course should be comfortable using a personal computer and Microsoft Windows XP or Windows Vista. Students will get the most out of this course if they want to learn the basics of Flash CS3 to create Flash applications for delivery on the Web.

Course objectives

You should share these overall course objectives with your students at the beginning of the day. This will give the students an idea about what to expect, and it will help you identify students who might be misplaced. Students are considered misplaced when they lack the prerequisite knowledge or when they already know most of the subject matter to be covered.

After completing this course, students will know how to:

- Identify the capabilities of Flash CS3 and the files it generates with an application, identify components of the Flash CS3 environment, and use the Help window.

- Create a new file from a template; set Stage properties; import images; create text blocks, drawing objects, and shapes; apply fills and strokes; transform shapes; combine objects and shapes; and create and reshape freeform shapes.

- Create, name, and manage layers; identify components of the Timeline; create frames, keyframes, and blank keyframes; and control the duration of a Flash application.

- Create custom colors and gradients; save custom swatches; and apply transparency, filters, and the Soften Fill Edges command.

- Create a frame-by-frame animation, create a motion tweened animation, control the acceleration and deceleration of a tweened animation, apply color effects, and create a movie clip animation.

- Create static buttons, rollover buttons, and invisible buttons; create a basic ActionScript; and apply a script to buttons to enable a user to control background music.

- Create content that's accessible to screen readers, optimize and test a Flash application to verify that it loads in a browser within a reasonable timeframe, and publish a Flash application as a SWF file and insert it into a Web page.

Skills inventory

Use the following form to gauge students' skill levels entering the class (students have copies in the introductions of their student manuals). For each skill listed, have students rate their familiarity from 1 to 5, with 5 being the most familiar. Emphasize that this is not a test. Rather, it is intended to provide students with an idea of where they're starting from at the beginning of class. If a student is wholly unfamiliar with all the skills, he or she might not be ready for the class. A student who seems to understand all of the skills, on the other hand, might need to move on to the next course in the series.

Skill	1	2	3	4	5
Opening Flash files and identifying interface components					
Manipulating elements on the Stage					
Using Flash Help					
Setting Stage properties					
Importing images					
Creating an expanding-width text block					
Creating a fixed-width text block					
Formatting text					
Toggling between text block types					
Drawing and formatting objects					
Combining shapes and drawing objects					
Creating freeform shapes					
Moving and reshaping with the Selection tool					
Reshaping with the Subselection tool					
Exploring marquee and lasso selections					
Creating layers					
Moving items to new layers					
Arranging and grouping layers					
Adjusting a layer's duration					
Creating custom color swatches					
Creating and applying gradients					
Applying filters					

Skill	1	2	3	4	5
Softening fill edges					
Creating frame-by-frame animation					
Creating a tweened animation					
Animating an alpha value					
Creating a looping animation					
Creating a button symbol					
Adding a movie clip to a button state					
Creating an invisible button					
Applying basic ActionScript commands					
Adding and controlling audio with ActionScript					
Creating accessible Flash content					
Setting the tab index					
Testing document download performance					
Publishing a SWF file					

Topic C: Classroom setup

All our courses assume that each student has a personal computer to use during the class. Our hands-on approach to learning requires they do. This topic gives information on how to set up the classroom to teach this course. It includes minimum requirements for the students' personal computers, setup information for the first time you teach the class, and setup information for each time that you teach after the first time you set up the classroom.

Hardware requirements

Each student's personal computer should have:

- A keyboard and a mouse
- An Intel Pentium 4, Intel Centrino, Intel Xeon, or Intel Core Duo (or compatible) processor
- At least 512 MB of RAM (1 GB recommended)
- 2.5 GB of hard disk space
- A CD-ROM drive for installation
- An XGA monitor set to a minimum resolution of 1024×768 (higher resolution recommended)

Software requirements

You will need the following software:

- Microsoft Windows XP with Service Pack 2 or Windows Vista Home Premium, Business, Ultimate, or Enterprise (certified for 32-bit editions); updated with the most recent service packs
- Flash CS3
- QuickTime 7 or later
- Internet Explorer

Network requirements

The following network components and connectivity are also required for this course:

- Internet access, for the following purposes:
  - Downloading the latest critical updates and service packs from www.windowsupdate.com
  - Downloading the student data files (if necessary)

First-time setup instructions

The first time you teach this course, you will need to perform the following steps to set up each student computer.

1 Install Windows XP on an NTFS partition according to the software manufacturer's instructions. If the student machines have Internet access, and they are behind a software or hardware firewall, install the latest critical updates and service packs from www.windowsupdate.com.

   Note: You can also use Windows Vista, although the screen shots in this course were taken in Windows XP, so students' screens might look somewhat different.

2 From the Control Panel, open the Display Properties dialog box and apply the following settings:

   • Theme — Windows XP

   • Screen resolution — 1024 by 768 pixels

   • Color quality — High (24 bit) or higher

3 Display file extensions and hidden files.

   a Start Windows Explorer.

   b Choose Tools, Folder Options and select the View tab.

   c Clear the check box for Hide extensions for known file types.

   d Select Show hidden files and folders and click OK.

   e Close Windows Explorer.

4 Ensure that sound is enabled, in order to complete Activity C-2 in the unit titled "Interactive components."

5 Install Adobe Flash CS3 according to the software manufacturer's instructions.

6 Start Adobe Flash CS3. Choose Help, Updates to open the Adobe Updater.

7 On the Adobe Updater, click Preferences. Uncheck Automatically check for Adobe updates. Click OK.

   Warning: The activities in this course were tested with updated software as of December 2007. If any subsequent Adobe updates include significant changes, some activities might not work exactly as described and some screen shots might not match what students will see on their screens. Therefore, if you choose to update the software, we strongly recommend that you go through the entire course, noting any changes so you can point them out during class.

8 Install the latest version of QuickTime (version 7 or later). The latest version can be downloaded from http://quicktime.apple.com. Accept all defaults during the installation.

9 Configure Internet Explorer to allow active content. This is necessary for several activities that preview animations in a Web browser.

   a Click Start, right-click the Internet Explorer icon, and select Internet Properties.

   b On the Advanced tab, under Security, check Allow active content to run in files on My Computer.

   c If you are using Internet Explorer 7, activate the Programs tab. Click Manage add-ons to open the Manage Add-ons dialog box.

   d Select Shockwave Flash Object in the Name list. Under Settings, select Enable.

   e Click OK. If a message box appears, click OK.

   f Click OK to close the Internet Properties box.

10 Create a folder called Student Data at the root of the hard drive (C:\).

11 If you don't have the CD that came with this manual, download the student data files for the course. You can download the data directly to student machines, to a central location on your own network, or to a disk.

    a Connect to www.axzopress.com.

    b Under Downloads, click Instructor-Led Training.

    c Browse the subject categories to locate your course. Then click the course title to display a list of available downloads. (You can also access these downloads through our Catalog listings.)

    d Click the link(s) for downloading the Student Data files, and follow the instructions that appear on your screen.

12 Copy the data files to the Student Data folder.

Setup instructions for every class

Every time you teach this course (including the first time), you will need to perform the following steps to set up each student computer.

1 If necessary, reset any defaults that you have changed. If you do not wish to reset the defaults, you can still re-key the course, but some activities might not work exactly as documented.

2 Delete the contents of the Student Data folder.

3 Copy a fresh set of data files to the Student Data folder. (See the download instructions in the preceding section.)

CertBlaster software

CertBlaster pre- and post-assessment software is available for this course. To download and install this free software, students should complete the following steps:

1 Go to www.axzopress.com.

2 Under Downloads, click CertBlaster.

3 Click the link for Flash CS3.

4 Save the EXE file to a folder on your hard drive. (**Note**: If you skip this step, the CertBlaster software will not install correctly.)

5 Click Start and choose Run.

6 Click Browse and then navigate to the folder that contains the EXE file.

7 Select the EXE file and click Open.

8 Click OK and follow the on-screen instructions. When prompted for the password, enter **c_flcs3**.

Topic D: Support

Your success is our primary concern. If you need help setting up this class or teaching a particular unit, topic, or activity, please don't hesitate to get in touch with us.

Contacting us

Please contact us through our Web site, www.axzopress.com. You will need to provide the name of the course, and be as specific as possible about the kind of help you need.

Instructor's tools

Our Web site provides several instructor's tools for each course, including course outlines and answers to frequently asked questions. To download these files, go to www.axzopress.com. Then, under Downloads, click Instructor-Led Training and browse our subject categories.

Unit 1

Getting started

Unit time: 30 minutes

Complete this unit, and you'll know how to:

A Identify the capabilities of Flash CS3 and the files it generates with an application.

B Identify components of the Flash CS3 environment.

C Use the Help window.

Topic A: Flash overview

Explanation

With Flash CS3, you can integrate text, images, video, and sound into your Web projects, and create animations and application interfaces. Any content you generate with Flash is called an *application*.

Types of Flash applications

You can use Flash to create a variety of applications, such as:

- Animations for Web page advertisements, promotions, and cartoons.
- Interactive games.
- Dynamic content sections, called *flexible messaging areas,* or *FMAs,* which are sections on a Web page that can change as necessary to provide up-to-date information to Web site visitors.
- User interfaces, such as Web page navigation bars.
- Rich Internet applications, which are applications that provide an interface for accessing and manipulating remote data.

Graphic content

Flash applications can include raster graphics and vector graphics. *Raster graphics,* such as GIF and JPEG images, consist of a grid of pixels and are common on the Web. Exhibit 1-1 shows an example of a raster graphic. If you enlarge or zoom in on a raster graphic, its pixels are clearly revealed.

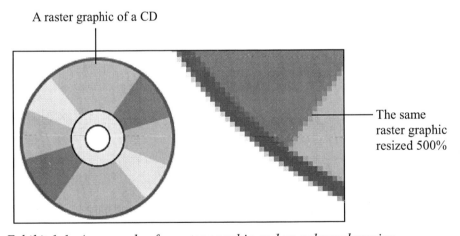

Exhibit 1-1: An example of a raster graphic and an enlarged version

Vector graphics are defined mathematically, and typically have smaller file sizes than comparable raster graphics. Flash incorporates vector graphics extensively to help keep file sizes small for faster download times. Exhibit 1-2 shows an example of a vector graphic. If you enlarge a vector graphic, there is no loss in quality or clarity. Therefore, vector graphics generate smoother animations than raster graphics do.

However, for *static images* (images that are not part of an animation or dynamic component), an optimized GIF or JPEG image typically has a smaller file size than a comparable static image in Flash format.

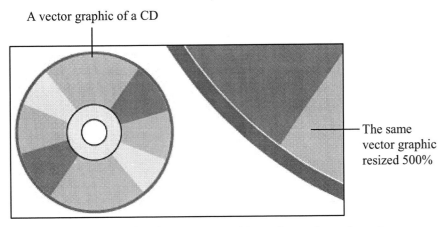

Exhibit 1-2: An example of a vector graphic and an enlarged version

Do it!

A-1: Discussing Flash concepts and applications

Question	Answer
1 If you need to create a complex animation for a product promotion, why might using Flash be better than an animated GIF?	*Flash files that are rich in graphics are typically smaller in file size, and therefore download faster.*
2 Native Flash files can contain both vector and raster artwork. True or false?	*True.*
3 What types of applications do you intend to create with Flash?	*Answers may vary.*
4 Flash is best for creating static artwork. True or false?	*False. Often, optimized GIF or JPEG images are best for ordinary static images.*
5 If you enlarge a raster image, it will not degrade in quality. True or false?	*False. Raster images typically appear pixilated when enlarged.*
6 If you enlarge a vector image, it will nct degrade in quality. True or false?	*True. Vector images do not consist of pixels, but are defined mathematically. Therefore, vector images resize gracefully, with no quality loss.*

Facilitate a brief discussion.

Opening Flash files

Explanation

Tell students they'll learn how to publish Flash files later in the course.

Flash applications have an .fla file extension. This is the raw Flash file that you create and modify in Flash. When you're ready to publish Flash content on the Web, use the File, Publish command to generate a finished, compressed version that has an .swf file extension, along with an HTML file to display the SWF file (commonly called a "swiff" file) in a Web browser. You can also play a SWF file in the Flash Player application, which is available free at www.adobe.com. If you need to edit a Flash file, you must open the FLA file.

Do it!

A-2:   Viewing Flash files

Here's how	Here's why
1 Use Windows Explorer to navigate to the current unit folder	In the Student Data folder.
Observe the files in this folder	There are four files: An editable Flash file, with an .fla extension; an exported SWF file, which will play in a Web page; and two HTML files, one of which contains a link to the SWF file.
2 In Windows Explorer, right-click **webpage.html**	
Choose **Open With**, **Notepad**	
Observe the code between the tags <!--AD PLACEHOLDER START--> and <!--AD PLACEHOLDER END -->	(Scroll down, if necessary.) Flash automatically writes this code, which embeds the SWF file for display in the Web page.
Close Notepad	
3 In Internet Explorer, open webpage.html	From the current unit folder.
4 Point to the ad	The pointer changes to a pointing finger when it's over the Click Here for More Info button.
Click the button	(The Click Here for More Info button.) To activate the link to the videos.html page, which appears in a second window.
Close both browser windows	
5 Click **Start**, and choose **All Programs**, **Adobe Flash CS3 Professional**	To start Flash CS3.
Observe the Welcome screen	The Welcome screen provides options for opening an existing file, creating a new file, or creating a new file using a template.
6 In the Open a Recent Item section, click **Open**	
Navigate to the current unit folder	
Select **outlandervideoad.fla**, and click **Open**	

Tell students that these are HTML comment tags, which allow you to notate your HTML markup.

If a security prompt appears at the top of the browser window, tell students to right-click the prompt and choose Allow Blocked Content, and then click Yes.

If the pointer doesn't change to a finger, have students click anywhere in the ad to activate it.

If the Product Activation screen appears, tell students to choose the trial option and click Continue.

Topic B: The Flash interface

Explanation

The Flash CS3 workspace, shown in Exhibit 1-3, includes a variety of tools, menu options, and other components that you can use to create Flash applications.

Tools panel   Timeline

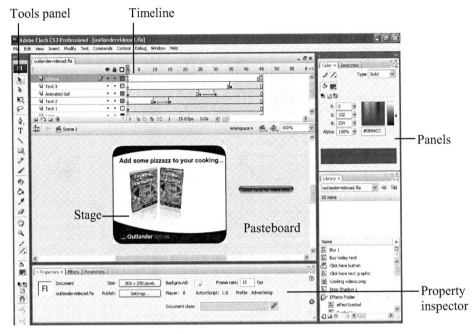

Exhibit 1-3: The Flash CS3 Professional interface

Flash window components

When you create or open a document in Flash, the Flash window is divided into five main components, which are described in the following table.

Component	Description
Stage/Pasteboard	The Stage is the main work area, where you place and view the graphics, video, and other visual elements of the application. The Stage represents a Web browser. If you place an object on the Stage, the object will appear in a browser in the final product. The space outside of the Stage is called the pasteboard. Items on the pasteboard are not visible in the finished product.
Timeline	The component you use to specify the timing of each element's appearance and animation.
Property inspector	Displays options that change according to the object that's selected.
Panels	Help you monitor, arrange, and modify media assets. You can show or hide individual panels by using the Window menu. The Library panel appears by default, and lists the graphics, video, audio, and other elements used in the current Flash document.
Tools panel	Contains tools you can use to create and modify vector graphic content.

The Tools panel

The Tools panel contains tools for selecting and editing shapes and images, applying and managing colors, and navigating.

The following table describes the functions of some of the more commonly used tools in the Tools panel.

Tool	Button	Description
Selection		Selects or moves an object
Free Transform		Transforms images, instances, or text blocks; you can resize, rotate, distort, or envelop images, instances, or text blocks
Text		Inserts a text block
Rectangle		Creates rectangles and squares
Pencil		Draws freeform lines and shapes
Paint Bucket		Changes the fill color of shapes; *fill* defines the color inside an object
Eraser		Erases unwanted parts of a shape
Zoom		Magnifies a particular area of a drawing

The Timeline

The Timeline is used to control the animation for each element (or group of elements) in the document. Each animated element is stored on its own layer, as shown in Exhibit 1-4. The Timeline also has a playhead, which acts like the needle on a record player. During playback, the playhead moves through the Timeline. When you're working in the Timeline, you can move the playhead to verify the content on the Stage at a particular point in the animation. To preview an entire animation, press Enter.

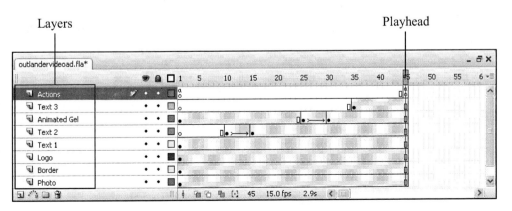

Exhibit 1-4: The Timeline

Objects drawn in Flash

A typical Flash file will contain a combination of elements, including objects drawn in Flash, text created in Flash, and imported graphics and sounds. When you use the drawing tools in Flash to create objects, they are *vector* objects.

After you create a vector object, you can easily modify it. For example, you can change the *fill color* (the color inside a shape) and the size of a vector object. You can also create text in Flash and apply formatting, such as the font face, size, alignment, and color.

Imported graphics and sounds

You can import existing vector graphics and raster graphics into Flash, as shown in Exhibit 1-5, such as pictures from a digital camera, scanned images, or images created in a photo editing application. In addition, you can import native Adobe Photoshop and Adobe Illustrator files into Flash.

You can also import PNG images created in Fireworks. If you import a Fireworks file as a flattened image, it is *rasterized*—converted to bitmap format. When you import a Fireworks file as an editable object, any vector content in the file remains in vector format.

You can also import sounds into Flash, such as background music or sound effects.

Exhibit 1-5: A Flash file with imported content and content created in Flash

ActionScript

ActionScript is the native scripting language of Flash. You can use it to add interactivity and to control events in your Flash application. Exhibit 1-6 shows a simple example of an ActionScript. The instruction shown opens a Web page when the user clicks a button.

```
1 animatedGel_mc.onRelease = function() {
2     getURL("site/videos.html", "_blank");
3 };
4
```

Exhibit 1-6: A simple example of ActionScript code

Do it!

B-1:   **Exploring Flash elements**

Here's how	Here's why
1 Press (↵ ENTER)	To preview the entire animation. The playhead in the Timeline begins moving to the right. When it reaches the end of the animation, it stops.
2 Drag the playhead back to the beginning of the timeline, as shown	
3 On the Stage, click the cookbooks	This is a raster graphic. It was imported into Flash.
4 Click the text at the top of the advertisement	This text was created in Flash.
5 Click the black border around the advertisement	The border was drawn in Flash.
6 Click the object on the pasteboard, as shown	
7 On the Timeline, scroll up to view the Actions layer	If necessary.
Click frame 1 of the Actions layer, as shown	
8 Choose **Window**, **Actions**	To open the Actions panel.
Observe the ActionScript code	This script opens the Web page videos.html when the button named animatedGel_mc is clicked.
Close the Actions panel	Click the × at the panel's top-right corner.

Point out that this is a raster graphic, and that the Photo layer is selected in the Timeline.

Point out that the Text 1 layer is selected in the Timeline.

Tell students that they will learn more about all these Flash elements later in this course.

Manipulating elements

Explanation

You can use the Selection tool to move and resize objects, and the Text tool to add or edit existing text.

To edit text:

1 On the Stage, double-click the text you want to change. This automatically selects the Text tool and places the insertion point in the text.

2 Edit the text as needed.

3 Select the Selection tool to finish editing the text.

Alignment guides

Alignment guides appear as you drag objects on the Stage. They allow you to align the center or edge of the object you are moving with the center or edge of other objects on the Stage. As you move an object close to an aligned position, alignment guides appear to help you position the object precisely, as shown in Exhibit 1-7.

The area of the image that snaps depends on which part of the object you use to drag. For example, if you drag an object from its top-left corner, that corner will snap, but if you drag from the center of the object, the center will snap.

To move items on the Stage:

• Using the Selection tool, drag the item you want to move.

• Click to select the item; then press the arrow keys on the keyboard to move the item one pixel at a time.

• Click to select the item; then enter values in the X and Y boxes in the Property inspector.

Exhibit 1-7: Alignment guides help you to position elements precisely

Do it!

B-2:   Changing elements on the Stage

Here's how	Here's why
1 On the Stage, double-click **Add some pizzazz to your cooking...**	To select the Text tool and to place the text insertion point in the text.
Edit the text to read **Give your cooking some pizzazz...**	
2 Select 	The Selection tool is on the Tools panel.
Point to the cookbooks image	
Drag the image to the left and up slightly to align it under the text, as shown	
3 Save the file as **My outlandervideoad.fla**	(Choose File, Save As.) In the current unit folder.

Topic C: Getting help

Explanation

You can use Flash's Help system to learn about Flash features, tools, and commands. You can find help topics by using a table of contents or a keyword search. In addition, you can limit your topics to certain Help books.

Flash Help

You access the Help window by choosing Help, Flash Help or by pressing F1. The left side of the Help window, shown in Exhibit 1-8, contains a search box, a Book list, and a list of topics. The right side of the window displays the selected Help topic.

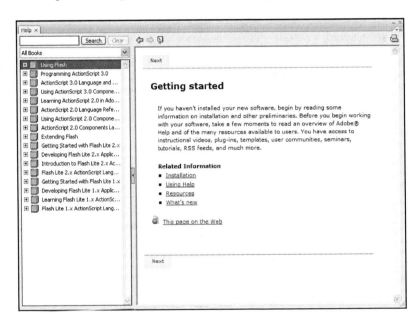

Exhibit 1-8: The Flash Help window

Do it!

C-1:   Using Flash Help

Here's how	Here's why
1 Choose **Help**, **Flash Help**	To open the Help window.
2 In the left pane, click the plus sign next to Using Flash	To expand the topic.
3 Expand the **Using Imported Artwork** subcategory	
4 Expand the **Placing artwork into Flash** subcategory	
5 Click **Importing file formats...**	To view this article. The contents of the article appear in the right pane.
6 In the Search box, enter **animated button** Click **Search**	(In the top left corner of the Help panel.) To search for Help topics that include these words.
7 Click **Apply a drop shadow**	(In the list of topics.) To view the information on this topic. Notice that both search terms are highlighted to help you locate them.
8 Close the Help panel	
9 Close the file	

TIPS
Tell students that they can also press F1.

Point out to students that they can resize the left pane to view the entire title of the article.

Unit summary: Getting started

Topic A   In this topic, you identified the types of applications that you can create in Flash. You also learned the difference between **raster graphics** and **vector graphics**.

Topic B   In this topic, you identified components of the **Flash interface**, and you moved an object on the Stage.

Topic C   In this topic, you learned how to use Flash's **Help system**.

Independent practice activity

In this activity, you'll open a Flash file, edit some text, and reposition one of the layout elements. You'll also search for help using the Help window.

1 In the Practice subfolder of the current unit folder, open quicknavigator.fla.

2 Save the file as **My quicknavigator.fla**.

3 Preview the animation. (*Hint:* Press the Enter key.)

4 Change the text "Navigation" to "Quick Navigation." (*Hint:* Double-click the word "Navigation" and enter the new text.)

5 Drag the Spices button to the left so that it follows the curve of the background image, similar to the example shown in Exhibit 1-9. (*Hint:* Use the Selection tool.)

6 Save the changes and preview the animation.

7 Open the Flash Help window and search for information about formatting text.

8 Close the Help window and close the My quicknavigator file.

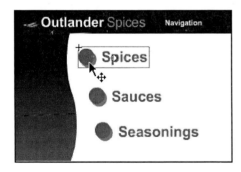

Exhibit 1-9: The layout after completing step 5 of the Independent practice activity

Review questions

1 Any content you generate with Flash is called:

   A A graphic

   B An interface

   C An animation

   D An application

2 Which of the following is true of raster graphics? (Choose all that apply.)

   A They're defined mathematically.

   B They're based on a grid of pixels.

   C GIF and JPEG images are raster graphics common to the Web.

   D They do not appear pixilated or blurred when resized or magnified.

3 What file extension do native Flash files have?

   A .swf

   B .fla

   C .jpg

   D .gif

4 Which are components of the Flash interface? (Choose all that apply.)

   A The Property inspector

   B The Timeline

   C The Tools panel

   D The Layers panel

5 Which of the following statements are true? (Choose all that apply.)

   A Items that appear on the Stage will appear in the finished application or animation, but items that are left on the pasteboard will not.

   B Items that appear on the pasteboard will appear in the finished application or animation, but items left on the Stage will not.

   C Items that appear on both the Stage and the pasteboard will appear in the finished application or animation.

   D The Stage is the main working area.

6 Which tool magnifies a particular area of a drawing?

  A Free Transform tool

  B Rectangle tool

  C Zoom tool

  D Selection tool

7 How can you preview an animation?

  A Press Enter.

  B Click Preview in the Property inspector.

  C Press Spacebar.

  D Press the Up arrow key.

8 Which are ways you can move an item on the stage? (Choose all that apply.)

  A Click to select the item; then enter values in the X and Y boxes in the Property inspector.

  B Click to select the item; then choose Modify, Move object. Enter values in the X and Y boxes, and then click OK.

  C Using the Selection tool, drag the item you want to move.

  D Click to select the item; then press the arrow keys on the keyboard to move the item.

9 To manually enter or edit ActionScript code, which panel do you use?

  A The Library panel

  B The Actions panel

  C The ActionScript panel

  D The CSS panel

Unit 2

Basic objects

Unit time: 120 minutes

Complete this unit, and you'll know how to:

A Create a new file from a template and set Stage properties.

B Import images into a Flash file and import items from another file's Library.

C Create fixed and expanding width text blocks and apply basic text formatting.

D Create, format, and manipulate drawing objects and shapes.

E Create and modify freeform shapes.

Topic A: New file settings

Explanation

When you create a new Flash file, you can either create a new blank file, or you can select a template containing settings such as Stage size and frame rate. When you create a file by using a template, the template you select will have preset Stage properties, including the Stage size, the background color, and the frame rate.

Stage size

The Stage size is measured in pixels. The advertising templates included with Flash correspond to standard ad sizes.

Frame rate

The playing speed of an animation is called the *frame rate*, and it's measured in frames per second (fps). This is the number of animation frames that play per second. The higher the frame rate, the faster the animation plays. Higher frame rates also increase the file size (and the resulting download time), and place a higher demand on the user's computer resources. Typically, the frame rate for a Flash application is 12 to 18 fps. This is slower than film or television frame rates, but fast enough to create a fairly smooth animation without taxing a computer's resources.

To create a new Flash file by using a template:

1   Choose File, New. The New Document dialog box opens.
2   Activate the Templates tab.
3   From the Category list, select the template category.
4   From the Templates list, select the template you want to use.
5   Click OK.

A-1: Setting Stage properties

Here's how	Here's why
1 Choose **File, New...**	To open the New Document dialog box.
Activate the Templates tab	
In the Advertising Category, from the Templates list, select **300x250 (Rectangle)**	
Click **OK**	To create a new file. You'll set several properties for the file.
2 Select the Selection tool	(If necessary.) To ensure that document properties appear in the Property inspector.
3 In the Property inspector, click the Size button, as shown	

Size: 300 x 250 pixels

Publish: Settings...

To open the Document Properties dialog box.

In the Title box, enter
Outlander video ad

In the Description box, enter
Medium rectangle ad for Cooking with Outlander video

Click **OK**   To apply the Stage properties.

4 In the Property inspector, in the Frame rate box, enter **15**   To increase the frame rate to 15 frames per second.

5 Choose **File, Save**   To open the Save As dialog box.

In the File name box, enter
MyVideoAd_objects

Navigate to the current unit folder

Click **Save**

Topic B: Library items

Explanation

You can use the Library to store symbols created in Flash, as well as imported images, sounds, and video clips. Whenever you import an image, sound, or video, it's automatically added to the Library. You can also convert objects created in Flash to symbols so they can be stored in the Library and re-used.

The Library panel

You can see which symbols and other objects are stored in the Library by viewing the Library panel. In the Library panel, you can organize items into folders, sort items by type, and see how often an item is used in a file.

Imported images

You can import images into a Flash file. You can import image file formats such as JPEG, GIF, and PNG, as well as native Adobe Photoshop and Adobe Illustrator files. When importing an image, you can choose to import an image to the Stage or directly to the Library. If you import an image to the Stage, it's placed on the Stage as well as into the Library as a graphic symbol. A *graphic symbol* is one of the three types of symbols (graphic, button, movie clip) in Flash. A *symbol* is a re-useable Flash element that is stored only once, but can be re-used as often as needed without significantly adding to the file size.

Importing to the Stage

To import an image to the Stage:

1　Choose File, Import, Import to Stage. The Import dialog box opens.
2　Navigate to the image you want to import and click Open. The image is imported to the Stage and is added as a graphic symbol in the Library so you can use it elsewhere in the Flash file.

Importing to the Library

If you import an image into the Library, it's imported as a graphic symbol and does not automatically get placed on the Stage.

To import an image to the Library:

1　Choose File, Import, Import to Library. The Import to Library dialog box opens.
2　Navigate to the image you want to import, and click Open. The image is imported into the Library as a graphic symbol.

Importing an external Library

You can also import elements from the Library of another Flash file. The ability to share common elements between files allows you to save time and ensure consistency in your Flash projects.

To import the Library items of another Flash file into the current Flash file:

1 Choose File, Import, Open External Library. The Open as Library dialog box opens.

2 Navigate to the Flash file containing the Library items you want to import and click Open. The Library panel from the external Flash file opens.

3 Drag the desired elements from the external Library panel to the current file's Library panel.

Importing TIFF images

The Tagged Image File Format (TIFF) is an image format used in print products. Web browsers do not support it. If you want to import TIFF images into Flash, you must also have QuickTime 4 or later installed on your computer.

Do it!

B-1: Importing images

Here's how	Here's why
1 Choose **File**, **Import**, **Import to Stage...**	To open the Import dialog box.
Select **Cooking DVD.jpg**	In the current unit folder.
Click **Open**	To import the image. This is an external graphic, so the image is also added to the Library.
2 Drag the image to the bottom-left side of the Stage, as shown	
3 Choose **File**, **Import**, **Import to Library...**	To open the Import to Library dialog box.
Import **Cooking VHS.jpg**	(In the current unit folder.) To import the image to the Library only.
Verify that the image appears in the Library panel	
4 Observe the Library panel	It contains several icons that represent various options available in the panel.
In the panel, select **Cooking VHS.jpg**	Icons in the panel that were dimmed are now active.

Tell students to drag the image so that its bottom border touches the bottom of the Stage.

5 Click as shown

To open the Bitmap Properties dialog box for the selected item.

Click **Cancel**

To close the dialog box.

6 Drag **Cooking VHS.jpg** from the Library to the Stage, as shown

Now you want to import the company logo, which is already in another Flash file. You'll get the logo from its library.

7 Choose **File**, **Import**, **Open External Library...**

You'll import the library of another Flash file.

8 Select **logoanimation.fla**

In the current unit folder.

Click **Open**

To open the file as a library.

9 Drag **logo** to the pasteboard, to the right of the Stage

To add it to the current library.

Observe the current file's Library panel

The logo image is added to the current file's library. The Logo rasters folder was also added, because it's a component of the logo object.

10 Close the Library panel for the logoanimation.fla file

11 Update the file

TIPS
Tell students that they can update a file by pressing Ctlr+S.

Topic C: Using text

Explanation

You can add text to a Flash application by using Flash's Text tool. In Flash, you can place text in either an expanding-width text block or a fixed-width text block.

Expanding-width text blocks

With an expanding-width text block, the width of the text block automatically changes as you type. To create an expanding-width text block, select the Text tool, click on the Stage, and type.

Do it!

C-1: Creating an expanding-width text block

Here's how	Here's why
1 Click a blank area of the pasteboard	To deselect the logo.
From the Zoom list, select **200%**	Workspace ▾ 🎬 🎬 200% ▾
	In the top-right corner of the work area.
2 In the Tools panel, click T	The Text tool.
Click the Stage near the top-left corner	To place the text insertion point.
Type **Give your cooking some pizzazz...**	Notice that the text block expands as you type.
3 Drag to select the text	Scroll to the left, if necessary.
4 In the Property inspector, from the Font list, select **Arial**	If necessary.
5 In the Font size box, enter **16**	
6 Click **B**	(If necessary.) To apply bold formatting.
7 Click the Text (fill) color icon, as shown	16 ▾ **B** *I* ≣ ≣ Anti-alias for Text (fill) color ▾
	To display the Text (fill) color list.
Select a black swatch	To apply black to the selected text.

Help students select the text, if necessary.

8 Select the Selection tool

Drag the text block to the indicated position

If necessary.

Fixed-width text blocks

Explanation

Fixed-width text blocks do not resize the width as the text is typed. The width is determined by the rectangle you draw with the Text tool. With a fixed-width text block, the text automatically wraps within the width of the text block.

Do it!

C-2: Creating a fixed-width text block

Here's how	Here's why
1 Click an empty area of the pasteboard	To deselect the text.
Select the Text tool	
2 Drag a text box on the Stage to the right of the images, as shown	To create a text block that has a fixed width.
3 Type **Buy Cooking with Outlander today!**	The text wraps within the block based on the width of the text block.

Point out that by default, the new text has the styles you applied last.

Text formatting

You can select various formatting options for text, including the font face, font size, type style (bold, italic), and color. You can also apply formatting to paragraphs of text, including alignment, margins, indents, and line spacing. You can apply formatting before or after you type your text.

To apply formatting to text before you type:

1 With the Text tool, click to create an expanding-width text block, or drag to create a fixed-width text block.

2 Choose the desired text formatting options.

3 Type the text. The text uses the formatting options you chose.

To apply text formatting after you type:

1 Create a text block and type the text.

2 Format the text by using either of these techniques:

- To apply formatting to the entire text block, select the text block with the Selection tool and choose the desired formatting options.

- To apply formatting to certain text within the block, select the text by highlighting it with the Text tool, and then choose the desired formatting options.

Anti-aliasing

Anti-aliasing smoothes the jagged edges of on-screen text. To turn on anti-aliasing for text, select the text and select an option from the Anti-alias list in the Property inspector. The option you choose will depend on the size and purpose of the text. For example, the Anti-alias for readability option and the Bitmap text (no anti-alias) option are usually good choices for small text, which can look blurry if smooth anti-aliasing is applied.

C-3: Formatting text

Here's how	Here's why
1 Select the Selection tool	
Click the right text block	(The one you last created.) To select it, if necessary.
2 In the Property inspector, in the Font size box, enter **18**	To set the font size for all the text in the text block.
Clear the bold formatting	Click the button in the Property inspector, or press Ctrl+Shift+B.
Select the Text tool	

3 Select the text **Cooking with Outlander**

Drag across the three words.

In the Property inspector, click I

To italicize the selected text.

Click the Text (fill) color swatch

From the Text (fill) color list, select a red swatch

To make the selected text red.

4 Click anywhere in the selected text

(If necessary.) To deselect it.

Click ¶

(On the Property inspector.) To open the Format Options dialog box.

Drag the Line spacing slider to 5 pt

To add vertical space between the lines.

Click **OK**

To close the dialog box.

5 In the Properties inspector, click ☰

To left-align the text.

6 Select the Selection tool

Drag the bottom-right corner handle to the left until each word appears on its own line, as shown

> Buy
> *Cooking*
> *with*
> *Outlander*
> today!

Tell students that they can click the pasteboard whenever they want to deselect an object.

Click the pasteboard

To deselect the text block.

Converting text blocks

Explanation

After you add text, you can convert an expanding-width text block to a fixed-width text block, and vice versa. To convert an expanding-width text block to a fixed-width text block, use the Selection tool to drag the top-right handle of the text block to the desired width. To convert a fixed-width text block to an expanding-width text block, double-click the top-right handle of the text block.

Do it!

C-4: Toggling between text block types

Here's how	Here's why
1 With the Text tool, click as shown	
	To insert an expanding-width text block in this location.
Type **Available on DVD or VHS**	The text is formatted automatically with the most recently applied text styles.
Select all the text and set it to 9 points	
2 Click	(In the Tools panel.) To select the Zoom tool.
Click the Stage	(If necessary.) To zoom in one level.
3 Using the Text tool, click within the text box	
Drag the top-right handle to the right edge of the image, as shown	
	To convert the text box to a fixed width, so that you can align the text below the two images.
In the Property inspector, click	(The Align Center button.) To center the text within the text box.
Click the pasteboard	To deselect the text box.

4 Create a fixed-width text block in the indicated position

Drag with the Text tool to draw the text block.

Type **Click here to shop or for more information**

The text wraps within the block. Again, the text is set automatically with the most recent text formatting you applied.

5 Double-click the square in the top-right corner of the text block

To convert the text block to an expanding-width block.

You now decide that you'd prefer it to fit on one line.

6 Edit the text to read **Click here for more info**

The text is now on one line, and the block changed width to accommodate the edited text.

Set the font size to 11 points

7 Update the file

Topic D: Basic shapes

Explanation

Flash provides several tools for drawing shapes, which you can combine and manipulate to create more complex objects and animations.

Drawing models

There are two drawing models available in Flash: the Object Drawing model and the Merge Drawing model. With the Object Drawing model, you can draw shapes as separate objects that do not automatically merge together when you overlap them. If shapes overlap, you can move them apart later or rearrange their stacking order. In the Merge Drawing model, you have to draw each shape on its own layer, or group shapes to overlap them without altering their appearance.

When you select an object drawn with the Object Drawing model, Flash surrounds it with a rectangular bounding box. You can use the Selection tool to move the object by dragging it anywhere you'd like to position it on the Stage.

To activate the Object Drawing model, choose the shape tool you want to use and click the Object Drawing button in the Tools panel to select it. Click the Object Drawing button again to activate the Merge Drawing model.

Fill and stroke colors

When you draw an object, the currently selected fill and stroke colors are applied to that object as you draw it. As shown in Exhibit 2-1, a *fill color* is the color inside an object, and the *stroke color* is the object's outline color. The last colors you selected will be applied by default, or you can select your own stroke and fill colors prior to drawing an object.

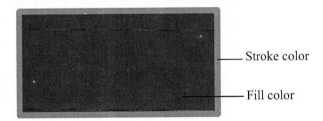

Stroke color

Fill color

Exhibit 2-1: Fill and stroke colors

To set the fill and stroke colors for an object, click the Stroke color box or the Fill color box, shown in Exhibit 2-2, and then click a desired color swatch from the palette that appears.

To draw a square, select the Rectangle tool, and hold down the Shift key when drawing. You can also draw a circle by selecting the Oval tool and holding down the Shift key as you draw.

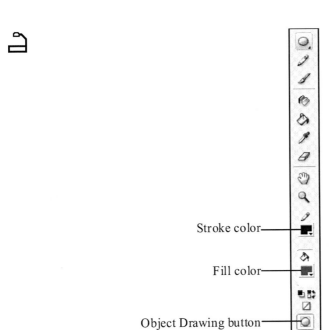

Stroke color

Fill color

Object Drawing button

Exhibit 2-2: The Tools panel, with the Oval tool selected

Do it!

D-1: Drawing objects

Here's how	Here's why
1 Choose **File, New...**	
Activate the General tab	
Verify that Flash File (ActionScript 3.0) is selected, and click **OK**	You'll create a new blank document.
2 Save the file as **My shapes.fla**	In the current unit folder.
3 In the Tools panel, click	To select the Rectangle tool.
In the Tools panel, click	(The Object Drawing button is located at the bottom of the Tools panel.) To keep overlapping shapes from interacting with one another.

4 In the Tools panel, click the Fill color box, as shown

To open the Fill color palette.

Select a blue color swatch

The fill color will appear inside the shape you create.

5 In the Tools panel, click the Stroke color box, as shown

Click as shown

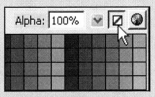

(The No color icon.) To specify that the shape will not have an outline.

The exact size isn't important, but have students keep the rectangle in the top quarter of the Stage.

6 Drag to create a rectangle approximately as shown

The rectangle appears with the selected fill color.

⚠ *If students point too close to the rectangle, the shape they'll draw will snap to its top right corner. If this happens, have them choose Edit, Undo Rectangle and redraw it.*

Tell students that the position of their square is unimportant.

7 Point to the right of the rectangle

You'll draw a square here.

Press (SHIFT) and drag

To create a square.

Release the mouse button and then release (SHIFT)

8 Hold down the mouse button on the Rectangle tool

(In the Tools panel.) To display additional tools.

Select **Oval Tool**

9 In the Tools panel, click the Fill color box and select a red color

10 Draw an oval below the rectangle

Tell students to keep the drawing objects in the top half of the Stage.

Create a circle to the right of the oval

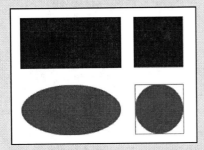

Hold down Shift and drag with the Oval tool.

11 Click the Fill color box and select a green color

(In the Tools panel.) To make the selected circle green.

TIPS
Tell students that they can also press Ctrl+Z to undo the last action.

Choose **Edit, Undo Fill Color**

To undo the last action.

Hold (CTRL) and click a blank area on the Stage

To temporarily access the Selection tool, which enables you to deselect the circle.

12 Click the Stroke color box and select black

13 With the Oval tool selected, point to the right of the circle, as shown

Press (ALT) + (SHIFT) and drag to the left

To create a green circle with a black stroke from the center outward.

Tell students that they can reposition the shapes in the top half of the stage by using the Selection tool.

14 Update the file

Selecting and formatting drawing objects

Explanation

After you create an object by using the Object Drawing model, you can change the fill or stroke with either the Tools panel or with the Property inspector, shown in Exhibit 2-3, which provides additional fill and stroke options.

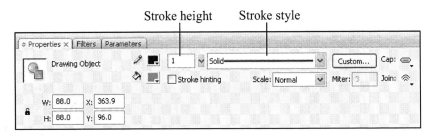

Exhibit 2-3: The Property inspector's stroke settings

Object stacking order

Flash stacks objects based on the order in which they were created, placing the most recently created object at the top of the "stack" of objects. This stacking order determines how your objects appear when they overlap, as shown in Exhibit 2-4.

You can change the stacking order of an object by selecting the object and choosing one of the commands in the Arrange submenu in the Modify menu.

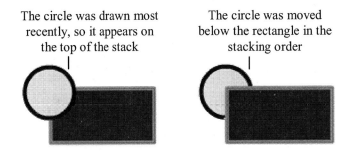

Exhibit 2-4: Object stacking order adjustments

By default, lines and shapes (drawn with the Object Drawing model disabled) always appear below objects (drawn with the Object Drawing model enabled), groups, and symbols in the stack. To move them up in the stack, you must group them or convert them to symbols.

The stacking order of a series of objects exists within a single layer, so anything on a layer above will be above all objects on a layer below.

Do it!

D-2: Formatting drawing objects

Here's how	Here's why
1 Select the Selection tool	If necessary.
2 Click the green circle	(If necessary.) To select it.

3 Observe the selection and the Property inspector

When an item drawn with Object Drawing mode is selected, a rectangular border appears around it, and it appears in the Property inspector as Drawing Object.

4 In the Property inspector, click the Fill color button and select a yellow color

To change the color of the selected object.

5 In the Stroke height box, enter **4**

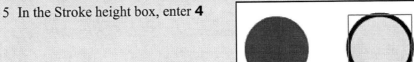

6 Select the rectangle in the top-left corner of the Stage

   Apply a gray stroke color

7 Drag the blue rectangle so that it partially overlaps the yellow circle

The circle appears in front of the rectangle. The more recently an object is drawn, the higher it appears in the stacking order.

   Choose **Modify**, **Arrange**, **Bring to Front**

The rectangle now overlaps the circle.

   Drag the red oval to partially overlap both the yellow circle and the blue rectangle

The oval appears behind the other shapes.

8 Choose **Modify**, **Arrange**, **Bring Forward**

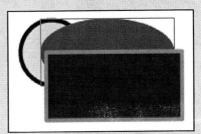

The oval moves one step up in the stacking order. The Arrange, Bring to Front command would have moved it to the top of the stacking order.

The Merge Drawing model

Explanation

The objects that you have drawn by using the Object Drawing model can be stacked and do not interact with one another. If you disable the Object Drawing model, the Merge Drawing model is enabled, and anything you draw is considered a shape, rather than an object. Any shapes that overlap one another will automatically merge and interact, while objects remain separate.

When you select an item, you can tell whether it's an object or a shape by viewing the item name in the Property inspector. When an object is selected, the words Drawing Object appear in the Property inspector. When a shape is selected, the Property inspector displays the word Shape.

Selecting shapes

If you draw an item by using the Object Drawing model, Flash treats it as an object. You can select an object by using the Selection tool.

However, when you use the Merge Drawing model to draw an item, Flash treats it as a shape, and clicking on various parts of the shape changes which component of the shape is selected. For example:

- Click the fill area of the shape to select only the fill.
- Double-click the fill area of the shape to select both the fill and the stroke.
- Click a stroke segment to select only that segment.
- Double-click a stroke to select the entire stroke.

Shape interaction

When you create items by using the Merge Drawing model, those items will interact with each other because they are shapes rather than separate objects. When two shapes of the same color overlap, they combine into a single shape. When two shapes of different colors overlap, the top shape creates a cut-out from the shape below.

Adding fills or strokes to shapes

If you originally drew a shape without either a fill or a stroke, you can't add a fill or stroke later by selecting fill or stroke settings in the Property inspector. Instead, you use the Paint Bucket and Ink Bottle tools.

- If the shape you drew didn't originally contain a fill, click inside the shape with the Paint Bucket tool to add a fill color.
- If the shape you drew didn't originally contain a stroke, click the edge of the shape with the Ink Bottle to add a stroke.

Do it!   **D-3:   Working with shapes**

Here's how	Here's why
1 Select the Oval tool	
2 Click	To disable Object Drawing and enable the Merge Drawing model.
3 Set the fill to blue and the stroke to None	In the Tools panel.
4 Draw two adjacent circles in the bottom-left corner of the Stage	
Change the fill color to green and draw a third circle	
Change the stroke color to black and draw a square	
5 Select the Selection tool	
Click the right blue circle	To select it.
Observe the selected shape and the Property inspector	A selected shape appears with a crosshatch pattern. The Property inspector indicates that this is a shape rather than a drawing object.

Have students keep shapes at the bottom of the Stage to more easily differentiate them from the drawing objects on the top half.

6 Drag the circle to partially overlap the other blue circle, as shown

Click the white space outside the circles

To deselect the shape.

Click either blue circle

In the Merge Drawing model, when you overlap shapes of the same color, they merge into a single shape.

7 Drag the green circle to partially overlap the blue shape

Click the white space outside the circles

To deselect the shape.

Drag the green circle away from the blue shape

In Shape drawing mode, overlapping differently colored items creates a "cut-out," removing the overlapping area in the lower item.

8 Click the middle of the green square

Clicking once in a shape with a stroke only selects the fill.

Drag the green square to an empty area

Only the fill color moves.

Choose **Edit, Undo Move**

To move the fill color back.

Step	Action	Result
9	Click the top edge of the green square's stroke	Only the top segment is selected because each segment of a stroke is considered separate when you draw in Shape mode.
	In the Property inspector, change the Stroke color to red	You can change each segment of a stroke individually.
	Double-click another edge of the square's stroke	Double-clicking selects all adjacent stroke segments of the same color, but not those of a different color.
10	Double-click the center of the green square	The fill and all stroke segments are selected.
11	Select the green circle	You will add a stroke.
	In the Property inspector, select a stroke color	The stroke color doesn't apply to the circle because a shape's fill and strokes are separate items, and this shape has no stroke to modify. You must use the Ink Bottle tool to add a stroke to a shape if none was originally present.
12	In the Tools panel, click [Ink Bottle icon]	The Ink Bottle tool.
	In the Tools panel, select a red stroke color	To choose the color the Ink Bottle tool will apply.
	Click the edge of the selected circle	To add a 4-point red stroke. The stroke height is based on the most recently applied stroke.
13	With the Selection tool, select the green square's fill	
	Press DELETE	To eliminate the fill. Much like adding a stroke when none is present, if you want to add a fill now, you need to use the Paint Bucket tool, not the Property inspector.
14	In the Tools panel, click [Paint Bucket icon]	The Paint Bucket tool.
	Select a green fill color	If necessary.
	Click the center of the square	To add a green fill.

Margin notes:

⚠ *Be sure students change the color in the Property inspector, not the Tools panel.*

TIPS ✔ *The "hot spot" of the tool is the bottom of the ink that appears to be flowing out of the bottle. This is important when you need to click in a precise spot.*

You could also select None for the fill in the Property inspector.

15 With the Selection tool, double-click the green circle with the red stroke

To select both the fill and stroke. You'll overlap this with a drawing object in the top half of the Stage.

Drag the selected circle to overlap it with the blue square near the top of the Stage

The shape appears behind the drawing object.

16 Choose **Modify**, **Arrange** and observe the submenu

The stacking order commands are dimmed, indicating that you can't move a shape above a drawing object.

Click a white area

To deselect the shape.

17 Double-click the circle

To select both the fill and stroke.

Drag the circle away from the square

The entire circle remains. Unlike when you overlap two shapes, overlapping a shape and a drawing object (or two drawing objects) doesn't create a cut-out or modify the original items in any way.

18 Update and close the file

Choosing between objects and shapes

Explanation

The following considerations can help you to decide whether to create an item as an object or a shape.

- Objects do not merge when overlapping, and are more easily selected than shapes. It's easier to change stacking order, and it's easier to change or add fills or strokes.
- Shapes are useful for combining objects, cutting out objects, eliminating parts of strokes, and so on.
- Legacy Flash files (prior to v8) contain only shapes, so you'll likely need to work with them even if you prefer to work with objects.

Making drawing objects act like shapes

Drawing objects are really "containers" for shapes. If you double-click a drawing object, you can edit it as you would a shape. This allows you to remove one segment of a stroke easily, for example. To return to the drawing object, click the current Scene tab above the workspace.

You can combine shapes simply by overlapping them. However, if you want to combine drawing objects, you need to choose a command from the Modify, Combine Objects submenu. The options are Union, Intersect, Punch, or Crop.

Making shapes act like drawing objects

If you group a shape (even by itself, without another item), you can prevent it from interacting with other shapes. Grouping a shape also allows you to control the stacking order for the shape.

If you place shapes on different layers, they will not interact with each other, so you don't need to worry about them overlapping.

Grouping objects

When you group objects, you can manipulate the grouped objects as a single object. When you select a group, the Property inspector displays the X and Y coordinates of the group and its pixel dimensions. To create a group, select the items you want to group and choose Modify, Group.

Transforming objects

Drawing objects are really "containers" for shapes. If you double-click a drawing object, you can edit it as you would a shape. This allows you to remove one segment of a stroke easily, for example. To return to the drawing object, click the current Scene tab above the workspace.

You can use the Free Transform tool to resize, skew, or rotate an object or shape. When using shapes, you will probably want to transform a shape before overlapping it with other shapes.

The following table demonstrates the types of transformations you can perform on a shape by using the Free Transform tool, and the pointer position necessary for each transformation type.

Type	Description
	To rotate an item, point to a spot just outside one of the corner handles until the pointer changes to a curved arrow and drag.
	To resize an item, point to one of the handles and drag. The corner handles enable you to resize horizontally and vertically at the same time.
	To move an item, point to the item—but not on the registration point in the center—and drag in any direction to move the item.
	To skew an item, point to a spot just outside one of the borders (not on a handle) and drag.

Do it!

D-4: Combining shapes

Here's how	Here's why
1 Create a new file by using the 300×250 (Rectangle) template in the Advertising category	Choose File, New, activate the Templates tab, select the template, and click OK.
Save the file as **My cutoutframe.fla**	(In the current unit folder.) You'll cut an oval shape from a rounded rectangle. This is straightforward to achieve with shapes.
2 Select the Rectangle tool	
In the Tools panel, set the stroke to No color and the fill to black	
Verify that the Object Drawing button is disabled	You'll draw in Shape mode.
3 In the Property inspector, click as shown	

	To display a slider. This is the Rectangle corner radius box.
Drag the slider up until the value in the box reads 20	To round off the corners of the rectangle you're about to draw.
Press ⏎ ENTER	

To apply the new setting.

4 Scroll to view the pasteboard on all sides of the Stage	If necessary.
Drag from the top-left corner of the Stage to the bottom right	

To create a rectangle that has rounded corners.

Deselect the rectangle

5 Set the fill color to red

To specify the color for the next shape you'll draw.

6 Select the Oval tool and draw an oval on the pasteboard, as shown

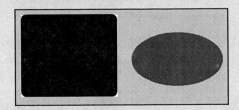

You don't want to draw it directly on the Stage because it would cut out part of the rounded rectangle. By drawing the shape here, you can size and rotate as desired first.

7 With the Selection tool, drag the oval so that it overlaps the rectangle

8 In the Tools panel, select [icon]

The Free Transform tool.

9 Drag the corner handles as necessary to size the oval approximately, as shown

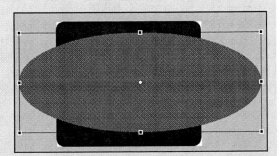

Point to the area just outside the top-right corner handle, as shown

The mouse pointer appears as a curved arrow, indicating that you can rotate the object.

Drag down slightly to rotate the shape clockwise

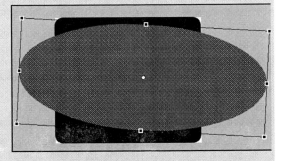

10 Deselect the shape

You need to deselect the shape to apply it.

Select the oval again

Now that the oval is applied, you can take action on it.

11 Press (*DELETE*)

To delete the oval, which leaves a cut-out in the rounded rectangle. You'll add 2 pixel vertical lines to each side of the rectangle.

12 In the Tools panel, select

The Line tool.

Set the stroke color to black and the stroke height to **2**

In the Property inspector.

13 Zoom in to 200% magnification

Help students with this step, if necessary. Tell them to start at the left edge of the top black section and drag downward to the bottom black section.

Drag as shown

To create a black border between the two black sections on the left side. The line snaps to the edge of the Stage.

14 Create a similar black line on the other side, as shown

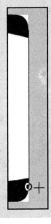

15 With the Selection tool, double-click the left line	To select it. If you single-clicked in the middle, the top and bottom segments where it touches the shapes would not be selected.
Press 	To nudge the line to the right so that it's completely on the Stage, and not halfway off on the left.
Double-click the right line and press	To nudge it onto the Stage.
Deselect the line	

Tell students to nudge the lines as needed.

This will serve as the boundary for an advertisement.

16 Update and close the document

Combining objects

Explanation

You can create complex shapes by combining or altering simple objects and using the commands in the Combine Objects submenu in the Modify menu. The following table outlines the Combine Object commands.

Command	Description
Union	Joins two or more objects into a single object.
Intersect	Creates an object from the intersection of two or more objects.
Punch	Removes portions of a selected object defined by a selected object on top in the stacking order.
Crop	Crops an object by using the shape of another object. The topmost selected object defines the crop area.

D-5: Combining drawing objects

Here's how	Here's why
1 Activate MyVideoAd_objects.fla	(If necessary.) You'll create a button with rounded left and right sides. You'll create this in Object Drawing mode with a Combine Objects command.
2 Select the Rectangle tool	
Set the fill to a blue color and the stroke to No color	
Set the corner radius to **0**	Enter 0 in the Rectangle corner radius box and press Enter.
3 Click	(On the Tools panel.) To switch to Object Drawing mode.
4 Drag a rectangle around the text **Click here for more info**	
5 With the Oval tool, draw a circle on the rectangle, as shown	
	Hold the Shift key to create the circle.
6 Switch to the Selection tool	
Drag the top center of the circle until it snaps to the corner of the rectangle, as shown	
7 Press and hold (CTRL)	Holding Ctrl while dragging an object creates a duplicate of the object.
Drag the circle to snap a duplicate on the right side of the rectangle	
Release (CTRL)	
8 Click the left circle	
Press and hold (SHIFT) and click the rectangle and the right circle	To select all three objects at once.
Choose **Modify**, **Combine Objects, Union**	To combine the three objects into one object.

Tell students to deselect the text box, if necessary.

Help students with the next few steps, if necessary. Remind them to hold the Shift key when creating the circle. Also tell them that it doesn't have to be positioned as shown here, because they can move it as needed.

9	Right-click the object	To display a shortcut menu.
	Choose **Arrange, Send Backward**	To move the shape behind the text.
10	Update and close the document	

Topic E: Freeform drawing and editing

Explanation

You can use Flash's Pencil tool to draw freeform objects or shapes. After you draw an item with the Pencil, you can edit the item by using the Selection or Subselection tools.

When using the Pencil tool to draw freeform objects or shapes, you drag the Pencil on the Stage, much like you would use a real pencil. You can use one of Flash's three drawing modes to assist you in drawing. You select a drawing mode from the Pencil Mode list at the bottom of the Tools panel. The following table describes the drawing modes available with the Pencil tool.

Mode	Effect
Straighten	Draws straight lines and allows you to create triangles, ovals, circles, rectangles, and squares when you draw an approximation of those shapes with the Pencil tool.
Smooth	Smoothes curves drawn with the Pencil tool.
Ink	Objects are drawn with no modifications to what you drew with the Pencil tool.

Do it!

E-1: Creating freeform shapes

Here's how	Here's why
1 Create a new Flash document with the default settings	Use the General tab of the New Document dialog box—not the Templates tab.
Save the document as **My leaf.fla**	In the current unit folder.
2 Select ✎	The Pencil tool.
3 Verify that Object drawing mode is active	
Click ⌐	(The Pencil Mode list.) To display a list of the three freeform options: Straighten, Smooth, and Ink.
From the Pencil Mode list, select **Smooth**	
4 Drag to draw the indicated shape	
	Flash automatically makes the line smooth when you finish dragging it. By intersecting the lines, you ensure that the area is closed, which will allow you to fill the shape with color. You'll address the extra line areas later.
Draw additional lines, as shown	
	To create the ribs of the leaf.
5 Update the file	

Tell students that their drawing does not need to look exactly like this one. They need to learn only the basics of how the Pencil tool works, not master it.

Also tell them that they can choose Edit, Undo or press Ctrl+Z to try again as needed.

The Selection tool

Explanation

Clicking an object (not a shape) selects the object completely, allowing you to move the entire object. When you use the Selection tool, if you click a line first to select it, dragging that line moves the line. However, if you don't select a line first, and then begin dragging it, you reshape the line. Even if a line is selected, dragging one of its endpoints changes the angle of the line.

Do it!

E-2: Moving and reshaping with the Selection tool

Here's how	Here's why
1 With the Selection tool, click the outline of the leaf	A selection box appears around the entire object. Only the outline is selected.
Zoom in to 200%	In the top-right corner of the workspace, from the Zoom list, select 200%.
2 In the Tools panel, click ⬓	(The Snap to Objects tool.) To disable object snapping, which will allow for more precise adjustments.
3 Drag the selected outline slightly to reposition it relative to the interior of the leaf	The outline of the leaf moves, but the lines inside it do not.
4 Deselect the outline	
5 Without clicking first, drag an edge of the leaf	To reshape the leaf's outline.
6 Double-click the leaf's outline	You'll edit its strokes as you would edit shapes.
Observe the bar above the workspace	"Drawing Object" appears, indicating that you're editing an object in place on the Stage.
Observe the strokes that form the interior of the leaf	The other items on the Stage are still visible, but they appear gray—deactivated.
7 Click the indicated segment of the leaf outline	To select it. When you edit shapes, parts of strokes beyond intersections are separate segments.
Press ⬓DELETE⬓	To delete this segment.
Delete the opposite segment	
8 Above the workspace, click **Scene 1**	To exit editing within the drawing object.
9 Update the file	

Tell students to drag from the outline. They can verify that they're about to move an object if the pointer appears with a four-sided arrow.

Tell students to focus on becoming familiar with how the tools work, and not on the quality of their drawing.

The Subselection tool

Explanation

You can use the Subselection tool to select and modify individual points on a path so that you can edit the path with precision.

Anchor points and direction handles

Paths created with the Pencil tool use anchor points and direction handles to determine the shape of the path. *Anchor points* are the points along the path, and *direction handles* control the amount of curvature of the path, as shown in Exhibit 2-5. A direction handle is composed of a direction line with a direction point at its end. To change the location of an anchor point or direction point, use the Subselection tool to select and drag it.

The farther a direction handle is from its anchor point, the more that segment of the path must curve in that direction before heading to the next anchor point.

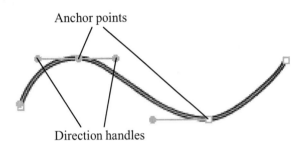

Exhibit 2-5: Anchor points and direction handles on a curve

Do it!

E-3:   Reshaping with the Subselection tool

Here's how	Here's why
1 In the Tools panel, click [➤]	(The Subselection tool.) You'll edit the points that comprise strokes with more control than is available with the Selection tool.
2 Click the line in the center of the leaf	Anchor points appear along the path.
3 Click an anchor point where the path curves gently	(Where it doesn't form a sharp corner.) To select a curve point.
Observe the direction handles	The direction handles extend from the point in a straight line with one another on opposite sides.
4 Drag the anchor point slightly to reposition it	The curve must pass through the anchor point, so it reshapes as necessary.
5 Drag one of the direction handles up or down to adjust the curvature of the path	The opposite direction handle remains in line with it, ensuring a smooth curve through the anchor point.
Drag a direction handle to lengthen or shorten the direction line	The attached segment bends as you drag. The longer the handle, the more the adjoining segment must curve in that direction prior to moving toward the next anchor point.
6 Click the outer leaf path	To display its anchor points.
Click the leftmost anchor point	
Observe the direction handles	The direction handles extend in different directions, not in a straight line with one another.
Drag the direction handles	The direction handles on a corner point work independently; each affects only one path segment.
7 Update the file	

Tell students that they will continue to become familiar with how the tools work. Tell them to not be concerned with the quality of their drawing.

If students select a corner point, have them try another point along the path, or along another path, such as the outside of the leaf.

Marquee selections

If you want to select portions of freeform shapes or a large group of items, you can create a rectangular selection marquee with the Selection tool, or use the Lasso tool to create an irregularly shaped selection area.

Selection tool marquee

You can drag with the Selection tool to create a rectangular selection marquee, allowing you to select multiple items, or a specific section of a freeform path (drawn in Merge Drawing mode), as shown in Exhibit 2-6.

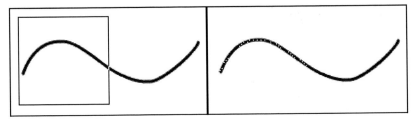

Exhibit 2-6: A selection marquee created with the Selection tool

Lasso marquee

You can use the Lasso tool to create an irregularly shaped selection, allowing you select areas that cannot be selected with the rectangular marquee.

E-4: Exploring marquee and lasso selections

Here's how	Here's why
1 Select the Selection tool	You'll select multiple objects within the leaf.
2 Drag a marquee, as shown	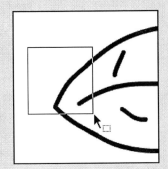
	To select a section of the leaf outline as well as a section of another line.
3 Release the mouse button	Each drawing object you touched with the marquee is selected. To gain further control over which items to select, you'll use the Lasso tool.
4 In the Tools panel, select 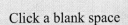	The Lasso tool.
Click a blank space	To deselect all objects.
Drag to select several of the leaf's ribs, as shown	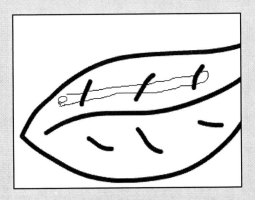
Release the mouse button	The ribs are selected.
5 Update and close the file	

Unit summary: Basic objects

Topic A   In this topic, you created a new file from a **template**, and you set **Stage properties** for the file.

Topic B   In this topic, you learned how to **import images** into a Flash file directly to the **Stage**, and also into the **Library**. You also imported items from another Flash file's library into the current file's library.

Topic C   In this topic, you learned how to create **fixed-** and **expanding-width text blocks**. You also applied basic **text formatting**, including font face, size, and style.

Topic D   In this topic, you created **drawing objects** and **shapes**. You also applied **fills** and **strokes**, and you **transformed shapes**. Then you combined drawing objects and shapes, and controlled shape interaction.

Topic E   In this topic, you learned how to create and reshape **freeform shapes**. You also learned how to select specific sections of a freeform shape, and use the Lasso tool to select multiple items.

Independent practice activity

In this activity, you'll create a Flash file with a specific Stage size, and you'll add elements to it to form the basis of a navigation system.

1. Create a new Flash file, and save it as **My quicknavigator** in the Practice subfolder in the current unit folder.

2. In the Property inspector, set the Stage size to **300×200 pixels** and the frame rate to **20 fps**.

3. Select the Rectangle tool and set the Rectangle corner radius value to 0.

4. In Shape drawing mode, create two shapes with black fills and no strokes, as shown in Exhibit 2-7.

5. Select the oval, and hold Ctrl as you drag to the right to make a duplicate.

6. Position one oval over the rectangle, as shown in Exhibit 2-8.

7. Select the second oval and change its fill to red.

8. Drag it over the rectangle, as shown in Exhibit 2-9.

9. Deselect the oval, reselect it, and delete it.

10. Zoom in to 200% and drag a marquee with the Selection tool, as shown Exhibit 2-10. Then press Delete to eliminate the part of the oval that hangs beyond the edge of the Stage.

11. Choose **File, Import, Open External Library** and import logoscale.fla. (*Hint:* The logoscale file is located in the Practice subfolder.)

12. Drag the Logo symbol from the logoscale.fla library to the top of the Stage, as shown in Exhibit 2-11. Close the Library panel.

13. Switch to Object Drawing mode and create a red circle, as shown in Exhibit 2-12. (*Hint:* Select the Oval tool and click the Object Drawing mode button.)

14. With the Text tool, add the word **Spices** to the right of the circle, formatted as Arial Bold at 20 points.

15 Add the text **Quick Navigator** near the top right, formatted as Arial Bold at 10 points, with a white fill.

16 Shift-click the circle and the word Spices, Ctrl-drag to duplicate twice, and edit the two copies to read **Sauces** and **Seasonings**, as shown in Exhibit 2-13.

17 Update and close the document.

Exhibit 2-7: The shapes as they appear after step 3

Exhibit 2-8: The shapes as they appear after step 6

Exhibit 2-9: The shapes as they appear after step 8

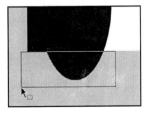

Exhibit 2-10: The selection marquee as described in step 10

Exhibit 2-11: The logo added to the Stage, as it appears after step 12

Exhibit 2-12: The Stage as it appears after step 13

Exhibit 2-13: The appearance of the Stage after step 15

Review questions

1 The Stage size is measured in:

   A inches

   B centimeters

   C points

   D pixels

2 The playing speed of an animation is measured in:

   A frames per minute (fpm)

   B frames per second (fps)

   C keyframes per minute (kpm)

   D keyframes per second (kps)

3   What is a symbol?

A   An icon you can use to create an interactive button

B   A re-useable Flash element that is stored only once, but can be re-used as often as needed without significantly adding to the file size

C   An icon that represents content on the Stage

D   A Flash object with no fill or stroke formatting you can use to affect animation without it being visible in the final output

4   Which are types of symbols? (Choose all that apply.)

A   graphic

B   button

C   text

D   movie clip

5   Which statements about importing images are true? (Choose all that apply.)

A   When you import an image to the Stage, it is also added as a graphic symbol in the Library.

B   When importing an image, you can choose to import an image to the Stage or directly to the Library.

C   When you import an image, you can determine which type of symbol to import the image as.

D   If you want to import TIFF images into Flash, you must also have QuickTime 4 or later installed on your computer.

6   How can you convert a fixed-width text block to an expanding-width text block?

A   Select the text block and choose Modify, Transform, Convert Text Block.

B   Right-click the text block and choose Modify, Transform, Convert Text Block.

C   Double-click the top-right handle of the text block.

D   Triple-click the text block.

7   How can you format all the text in a text block? (Choose all that apply.)

A   Select all the text in the text block by using the Text Tool; then choose the desired formatting options.

B   Right-click the text block and choose Format All Text; then choose the desired formatting options.

C   Select the text block with the Selection tool and choose the desired formatting options.

D   Select the text block, choose Text, Format All Text, and choose the desired formatting options.

8 Which anti-aliasing options are good for small text? (Choose all that apply.)

   A anti-alias for readability

   B anti-alias for animation

   C bitmap text (no anti-alias)

   D use device fonts

9 Which statements about the Object Drawing model are true? (Choose all that apply.)

   A You can draw shapes as separate objects that do not automatically merge together when you overlap them.

   B When you select an object drawn with the Object Drawing model, Flash surrounds it with a rectangular bounding box.

   C You have to draw each shape on its own layer or group shapes to overlap them without altering their appearance.

   D To activate the Object Drawing model, choose the shape tool you want to use and click the Object Drawing button in the Tools panel.

10 Which of the following statements about stacking order are true? (Choose all that apply.)

   A Flash stacks objects based on the order in which they were created, placing the most recently created object at the top of the "stack" of objects.

   B Flash stacks objects based on the order in which they were created, placing the most recently created object at the bottom of the "stack" of objects.

   C The stacking order of a series of objects exists within a single layer, so anything on a layer above will appear above all objects on a layer below.

   D The stacking order of a series of objects exists within a single layer, so anything on a layer above will appear underneath all objects on layers below.

11 When combining objects, the Union command:

   A creates an object from the intersection of two or more objects.

   B joins two or more objects into a single object.

   C crops an object by using the shape of another object. The topmost selected object defines the crop area.

   D removes portions of a selected object defined by a selected object on top in the stacking order.

12 When combining objects, the Intersect command:

   A creates an object from the intersection of two or more objects.

   B joins two or more objects into a single object.

   C crops an object by using the shape of another object. The topmost selected object defines the crop area.

   D removes portions of a selected object defined by a selected object on top in the stacking order.

13 When combining objects, the Punch command:

   A creates an object from the intersection of two or more objects.

   B joins two or more objects into a single object.

   C crops an object by using the shape of another object. The topmost selected object defines the crop area.

   D removes portions of a selected object defined by a selected object on top in the stacking order.

14 When combining objects, the Crop command:

   A creates an object from the intersection of two or more objects.

   B joins two or more objects into a single object.

   C crops an object by using the shape of another object. The topmost selected object defines the crop area.

   D removes portions of a selected object defined by a selected object on top in the stacking order.

Unit 3

The Timeline

Unit time: 45 minutes

Complete this unit, and you'll know how to:

A Use layers to manage content in a Flash application.

B Add frames and keyframes to the Timeline.

Topic A: Layers

Explanation

When you create a new Flash document, it contains only one layer. You can add more layers as needed to organize artwork, animation, and other components of your project.

Creating layers

You can create several layers in your Flash files to help you manage drawing objects, shapes, text, and other elements that will appear on the Stage. If you plan to animate items, each item you want to animate needs to be placed on a separate layer.

To create a layer:

1 In the Timeline, select the layer below where you want the new layer to appear.
2 Click the Insert Layer button. Flash creates a new layer above the currently selected layer.
3 Double-click the name of the new layer.
4 Type a name for the layer and press Enter.

Do it!

A-1: Creating layers

Here's how	Here's why
1 Open videoad_timeline.fla	From the current unit folder.
Save the file as **My videoad_timeline.fla**	
2 In the Timeline, click 🖼	(The Insert Layer button.) To create a new layer.
In the Timeline, double-click the layer name	To highlight it for editing.
Type **Logo** and press ⏎ ENTER	To rename the layer.
3 Add a new layer	Click the Insert Layer button.
Name the layer **Photo**	Double-click the layer, type Photo, and press Enter.
4 Add another layer named **Button**	
Add three layers: **Text 1**, **Text 2**, and **Text 3**	You'll move each object into its own layer.

5 Drag the border at the bottom of
the Timeline downward, as shown

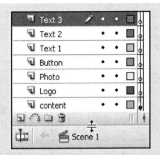

To view all of the layers without needing to
scroll.

Placing items on different layers

Explanation

If you already have items on a single layer, you can create new layers and then move the
items onto those new layers. You can also hide and show the contents of layers to make
it easier to work with overlapping contents.

To move an item to a new layer:

1 Select an item.
2 Choose Edit, Cut.
3 Select the layer on which you want to place the item.
4 Choose Edit, Paste to have the item appear in the center of the layer, or choose
Edit, Paste in Place to have the item appear in its original location on the Stage.

Hiding and showing layers

To make it easier to work with overlapping contents in multiple layers, you can hide and
show each layer's contents. Next to the layer, click the dot in the Hide/Show column to
hide it, and click the × next to a hidden layer to show it.

A-2: Moving items to new layers

Here's how	Here's why
1 With the Selection tool, click the Outlander Spices logo	
Choose **Edit**, **Cut**	
2 In the Timeline, click the logo layer	To select it.
3 Choose **Edit**, **Paste in Place**	To paste the logo into the Logo layer, in its same location on the Stage.
4 Move the blue button to the Button layer	Select the button and choose Edit, Cut. Click the Button layer and choose Edit, Paste in Place.
Move the photo to the Photo layer	The white space at the bottom of the photos partially obscures the logo, which is in a layer below. You'll fix this problem shortly.
Move the text **Give your cooking some pizzazz...** to the Text 1 layer	
Move the text **Buy Cooking with Outlander today!** to the Text 2 layer	
5 Click the Show/Hide column next to the Photo layer, as shown	

	To hide the Photo layer and its contents.
Move the text **Available on DVD or VHS** to the Text 3 layer	
Click the Show/Hide column next to the Photo layer again	To show the Photo layer and its contents.
6 Click each of the layers	Selecting a layer selects the object(s) on that layer.
7 Update the file	

Be sure students don't choose the Paste command; doing so will reposition the item on the Stage.

TIPS *You might suggest that students use the shortcuts Ctrl+X for the Cut command and Ctrl+Shift+V for the Paste in Place command.*

You want to select the text Available on DVD or VHS, but it's hidden by the photo.

Managing layers

Explanation

You can rearrange layers in the layer list, delete layers that you don't need, and organize layers into folders to make it easier to work with a large number of layers.

Moving layers

To move a layer, drag its name up or down in the layer list and release the mouse button when the line appears in the desired position in the list.

Deleting layers

To delete a layer, select it in the layer list and click the Delete Layer button.

Layer folders

When you have a large number of layers, it is often easier to manage them if you group related layers and organize them into named folders.

To group layers into folders:

1 Click the Insert Layer Folder button to create a new layer folder.
2 Name the layer folder and move it to the desired position in the layer list.
3 Drag the icon of each layer you want in the group to the icon of the layer folder.

Do it!

A-3: Arranging and grouping layers

By default, Flash documents created with a template in the Advertising category contain a layer named "content."

Here's how	Here's why
1 Click the content layer	(If necessary.) To designate where a new layer would be placed in the stacking order. New layers are inserted above the currently selected layer.
Create a new layer named **Border**	The Border layer appears above the content layer.
2 Open cutoutframe.fla	From the current unit folder.
3 In the Timeline, select the content layer	To select the contents of that layer.
Choose **Edit**, **Copy**	
4 Close cutoutframe.fla	
5 Choose **Edit**, **Paste in Place**	The white space below the photo obscures the border. You'll rearrange the layers so that the border and logo are above the photo.

6 Drag the Photo layer below the
   Border layer, as shown

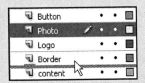

As you drag, a line appears to indicate where the
layer will be placed.

Release the mouse button

To move the Photo layer below the Border layer.
You'll combine the contents of the Logo,
Border, and Photo layers, because all of those
elements will be on the Stage for the duration of
the animation you'll create.

7 Select the Border layer

Before moving the border to another layer,
you'll group its contents, which will allow it to
be above other items in the same layer.
(Ungrouped shapes always appear behind other
items.)

TIPS
  *They can also
press Ctrl+G.*

Choose **Modify**, **Group**

8 Hold (SHIFT) and select the Logo
   layer

To select the contents of both the Border and
Logo layers.

Cut the selected contents

Paste the contents in place into the
Photo layer

Select the Photo layer and choose Edit, Paste in
Place.

9 Rename the Photo layer
   Background

10 Click the pasteboard

(If necessary.) To deselect any selected frames.

*Direct students to the
location of frame 1, and
tell students they will learn
more about the Timeline
and its components
shortly.*

11 Observe frame 1 for each layer

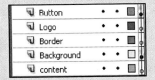

The Logo, Border, and content layers are now
all empty, as designated by the white frames
with hollow circles.

12 Click the content layer

To select it.

Hold (CTRL) and click the Border
layer

So that you can select non-adjacent layers.

Hold (CTRL) and click the Logo
layer

You'll combine the three text layers into a layer folder that you can collapse to reduce the height of the Timeline.

13 Click 🗑

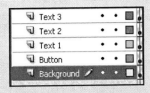

(The Delete Layer button.) To delete the unneeded layers. The Text layers, Button layer, and Background layer remain.

14 Select the Text 3 layer

Click 🗀

(The Insert Layer Folder button.) To create a layer folder above Text 3.

Rename the folder **Text**

15 Select the Text 1 layer

Hold ⸤ SHIFT ⸥ and click the Text 3 layer

Shift-clicking a layer selects the range of layers between it and the previously selected layer. All three text layers are selected.

Drag one of the selected layers to the Text layers folder

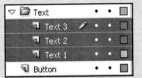

To move the layers into the folder. The layers are indented under the Text folder to indicate that they're inside that folder.

16 Click the triangle to the left of the folder icon

To collapse the folder, hiding its layers.

Expand the Text layers folder

Click the triangle to its left.

17 Update the file

Topic B: Timeline basics

Explanation Although you can use Flash's Timeline to arrange content into layers, you can also use the Timeline to control content over time. You can set the duration of the Flash application by adding frames to the Timeline, and you can control the sequence and timing of events by creating keyframes.

When you create a new Flash file, its duration is one frame. You can add frames to layers to increase the duration of that layer. The actual time duration depends on the frame rate of the application. For example, if the frame rate is set to 15 frames per second, 30 frames would be two seconds in duration. It would be slightly longer if the frame rate were 12 frames per second.

Frames, keyframes, and blank keyframes

The Timeline can consist of frames, keyframes, and blank keyframes, as shown in Exhibit 3-1. Each frame on the Timeline is like a slide in a filmstrip, or a page in a cartoon flipbook. To add frames to the Timeline, click or drag in the frame grid where you want to add frames and choose Insert, Timeline, Frame.

A *keyframe*, which is indicated by a black circle on a frame, defines the moment in the animation where an action of some kind occurs. For example, a keyframe could define when an object appears on the Stage during playback, or it could define when a sound file begins playing. To add a keyframe, click in the frame grid and choose Insert, Timeline, Keyframe. To move a keyframe, click the keyframe, release the mouse button, click again, and drag it to a new position on the Timeline.

A *blank keyframe*, which is represented by a white circle on a frame, does not yet contain any content. To add a blank keyframe, click in the frame grid and choose Insert, Timeline, Blank Keyframe.

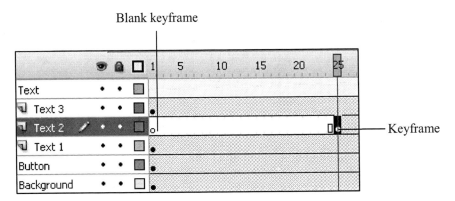

Exhibit 3-1: The Timeline

Do it!

B-1:   Adjusting a layer's duration

Here's how	Here's why

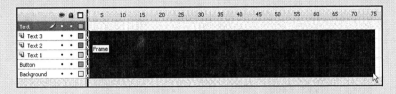

You want this application to be about 5 seconds long, which at 15 frames per second requires 75 frames.

1 Drag from frame 2 of the Text 3 layer down and to the right to frame 75 of the Background layer

The application's frame rate is 15 fps, and you want the application to run for 5 seconds.

Or press F5.

Choose **Insert**, **Timeline**, **Frame**

To increase the duration of all of the layers to 75 frames.

2 Click frame 1 of the Text 2 layer

To select the keyframe in frame 1 of that layer.

In the Text 2 layer, drag frame 1 to frame 25, as shown

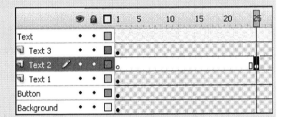

The contents of the Text 2 layer will appear beginning on frame 25, before two seconds have elapsed in the playback.

Remind students to release the mouse button before clicking and dragging the keyframe.

3 Make the button layer start at frame 45

Click frame 1 of the Button layer. Drag the keyframe in frame 1 to frame 45.

4 Make the Text 3 layer start at frame 60

Tell students that the red bar on the Timeline is called the playhead, and it's like the needle on a record player.

5 Above all the layers, click frame 1 in the Timeline, as shown

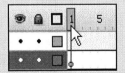

To move the playhead to the beginning of the animation. The playhead indicates the current position of the playback, and is similar in concept to a needle on a record player.

Press ⏎ ENTER

To play the animation. As the application plays, the Buy Cooking with Outlander text appears, then the button appears, and then "Available on DVD or VHS" appears.

Play the application again

Press Enter.

6 Update and close the file

Unit summary: The Timeline

Topic A   In this topic, you learned how to use **layers** to manage content in a Flash application. You learned how to create and name layers, and show and hide layers. Then you learned how to move content to separate layers, **rearrange layers**, and **delete layers**. You also learned how to **group layers** and organize them in a **layer folder**.

Topic B   In this topic, you learned the basics of the **Timeline**, including **frames**, **keyframes**, and **blank keyframes**. You learned how to use the Timeline to set the duration of a Flash application and control the appearance of content over time.

Independent practice activity

In this activity, you'll create layers and adjust their keyframes to make some objects appear on the Stage later as the application plays.

1 Open quicknavigator.fla from the Practice subfolder in the current unit folder, and save it as **My quicknavigator.fla**.

2 Create layers named **Sauces**, **Spices**, and **Seasonings**.

3 Rename Layer 1 **Background**.

4 Arrange the layer order as shown in Exhibit 3-2.

5 Select the word **Spices** and the circle to its left, cut them from the Background layer, and paste them in place in the Spices layer. (*Hint:* Use the Paste in Place command.)

6 Move the other two words and circles to their respective layers.

7 In the Timeline, drag through all four layers in frame 40, and choose **Insert**, **Timeline**, **Frame**.

8 Click the first keyframe in the Spices layer and drag it to frame 17.

9 Position the first keyframes of the Sauces and Seasonings layers at frames 20 and 23, as shown in Exhibit 3-3.

10 Click frame 1 and press Enter to play the application. Each word should appear in succession.

11 Update and close the file.

Exhibit 3-2: The layer order at the end of step 4

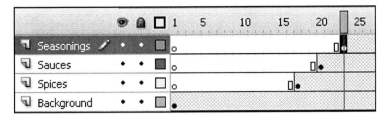

Exhibit 3-3: The Timeline as it appears after step 9

Review questions

1 If you have several layers, it's often helpful to:

   A delete them.

   B rearranges them alphabetically.

   C group related layers and organize them into named folders.

   D save the layers to an external file.

2 You can control the duration of an animation by:

   A inserting keyframes.

   B adding frames to the Timeline.

   C specifying the time limit in the Property inspector.

   D specifying the Stage settings.

3 You can set the speed with which an animation runs by:

   A changing the frames per second value in the Property inspector.

   B changing the frames per second in the Document Properties dialog box.

   C specifying the speed for each frame individually.

   D changing the frames per second value in the Timeline.

4 A keyframe is:

   A represented by a white circle on a frame, and defines a frame that does not yet contain any content.

   B indicated by a white circle on a frame, and defines the moment in the animation where change of some kind occurs.

   C represented by a black circle on a frame, and defines a frame that does not yet contain any content.

   D indicated by a black circle on a frame, and defines the moment in the animation where change of some kind occurs.

5 A blank keyframe is:

   A represented by a white circle on a frame, and defines a frame that does not yet contain any content.

   B indicated by a white circle on a frame, and defines the moment in the animation where change of some kind occurs.

   C represented by a black circle on a frame, and defines a frame that does not yet contain any content.

   D indicated by a black circle on a frame, and defines the moment in the animation where change of some kind occurs.

Unit 4

Formatting objects

Unit time: 45 minutes

Complete this unit, and you'll know how to:

A Create custom colors and gradients, and save them as swatches for repeated use.

B Create soft edges for objects by using a filter, and apply the Soften Fill Edges command.

Topic A: Custom colors and gradients

Explanation

In Flash, you can create your own colors and gradients to more precisely fit your needs.

Custom colors

You can define custom colors and save them as color swatches for repeated use. You create custom color swatches by using the Color dialog box. You can define a color by using either the HSL or RGB color models. The *HSL color model* is based on the hue (a particular color within the spectrum), saturation (the intensity of the hue), and luminosity (the amount of light in the color). The *RGB color model* is based on the intensity of red, green, and blue in the color.

You can also set the alpha value for a color. *Alpha* is the amount of opacity or transparency of a color. A value of 0% is fully transparent and a value of 100% is fully opaque. There are two methods that you can use to define a custom color.

To define a custom color with the Color dialog box:

1 In the Tools panel, click the Fill Color or Stroke Color button to open the Color palette.
2 Click the Color icon to open the Color dialog box.
3 Enter values in the Hue, Sat, and Lum boxes or the Red, Green, and Blue boxes to define a color.
4 Click OK.

To define a custom color with the Color panel:

1 Activate the Color panel.
2 Enter values in the R, G, and B boxes.

To save a custom color as a swatch:

1 Define a custom color with the Color dialog box or Color panel.
2 In the Color panel, set an alpha value if you want the color to have a degree of transparency.
3 From the Color panel Options menu, choose Add Swatch. The swatch is now available in the Swatches panel or within the Color palette.

Do it!

A-1: Creating custom color swatches

Here's how	Here's why
1 Open videoad.fla	From the current unit folder.
Save the file as **My videoad.fla**	
2 On the Text 2 layer, select the keyframe at frame 25	To display and select the content of that layer.
With the Text tool, select the text **Cooking with Outlander**	You'll apply an orange color similar to the word Spices in the company's logo.
3 Activate the Color panel	If necessary.
4 From the Type list, select **Solid**	If necessary.
Enter the following values: R: **255**, G: **100**, B: **0**	
With the Selection tool, click outside the Stage	(To deselect the text.) The text now appears in the orange color you defined.

Be sure that no items are selected before this step.

5 From the Color panel Options menu, choose the indicated option	
	To add the custom orange color you defined.
Activate the Swatches panel	The orange color you defined has been added as a swatch at the bottom-left corner of the solid color swatches.
6 Activate the Color panel	
Define a blue color with the following values: R: **0**, G: **0**, B: **185**	
In the Alpha box, enter **60**	This color will be 60% opaque.
7 From the Color panel Options menu, choose **Add Swatch**	
Activate the Swatches panel	The semi-transparent blue color appears to the right of the orange swatch you created.

8	Select the opening keyframe of the Button layer	(Frame 45 in the Button layer.) To select that keyframe and the button itself.
9	With the Selection tool, double-click the button	The other items on the Stage dim, indicating that they won't be edited.
	Click near the right rounded edge	To select the shape.
	In the Swatches panel, click the custom blue swatch	
	At the top of the workspace area, click **Scene 1**	To go back to editing the main Timeline.
10	Drag the button partly over the photo	To observe the transparency. You can use transparency to create a variety of effects in your Flash applications.
	Choose **Edit**, **Undo Move**	To return the button to its original location.
11	Update the file	

⚠ *If the color is not applied properly, have students click a different swatch, and then the blue swatch.*

Tell students to zoom in to see the effect more clearly, if needed.

Custom gradients

Explanation

In the same way that you can define solid colors and save them as swatches for later use, you can also create gradients. A *gradient* is a fill that gradually changes from one color or shade to another. You can also create gradients that include transparency, and that include up to 15 color transitions.

You can create either linear or radial gradients. A *linear gradient* changes color along a single axis, and a *radial gradient* changes color from a specific point outward, as shown in Exhibit 4-1.

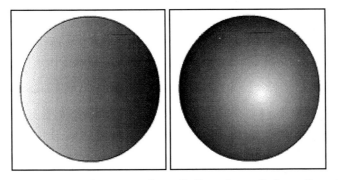

Exhibit 4-1: A linear gradient (left) and a radial gradient (right)

To create a custom gradient:

1 Activate the Color panel.

2 From the Type list, select a gradient type (linear or radial).

3 Click the starting gradient color swatch to select it. In the Color panel, enter the desired RGB values and/or alpha value.

4 Click the ending gradient color swatch. In the Color panel, enter the desired RGB values and/or alpha value.

5 Add additional colors to the gradient by clicking just below the color ramp to create a new gradient swatch. Click it and set the desired RGB values and/or alpha value.

6 If necessary, you can remove a color from the gradient by dragging its swatch away from the color ramp.

To create a gradient based on existing colors in the color palette, you can double-click a color gradient swatch to open the color palette and then select a color.

The Gradient Transform tool

You can transform a gradient fill by adjusting the size, direction, or center of the fill by using the Gradient Transform tool.

The control handles for the Gradient Transform tool change depending on whether you have a linear gradient (shown in Exhibit 4-2) or a radial gradient (shown in Exhibit 4-3) applied to an object.

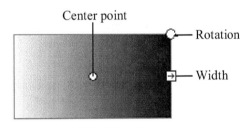

Exhibit 4-2: A linear gradient selected with the Gradient Transform tool

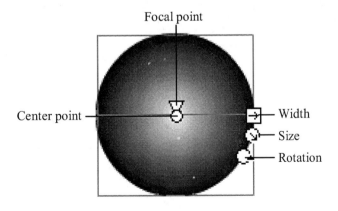

Exhibit 4-3: A radial gradient selected with the Gradient Transform tool

A-2: Creating and applying gradients

Here's how	Here's why
1 With the Selection tool, double-click the button	To edit the components within the group separately, without ungrouping them. The rest of the items on the Stage are dimmed, indicating that they won't be edited.
Zoom in to 200%	
Click near the right rounded edge	(If necessary.) To select the object.
2 Activate the Color panel	
3 From the Type list, select **Linear**	To view the gradient settings.
4 Click the starting gradient color swatch, as shown	

You'll set a custom starting color for this gradient.

Enter the following values: R: **0**, G: **0**, B: **80**	In the Color panel.
Click the ending gradient color swatch	

You'll define the ending gradient color.

Enter the following values: R: **0**, G: **204**, B: **255**	
5 In the Tools panel, hold down the mouse button on the Free Transform tool	To display additional tools.
Select the Gradient Transform tool	
Drag the ➡ handle from the right edge of the button to the right of the center mark, as shown	

6 Drag the  handle downward, to rotate the gradient 90 degrees clockwise

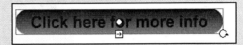

   Drag the bottom edge of the gradient upward, to snap to the edge of the drawing object

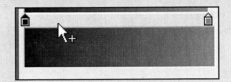

You'll add another color within the gradient to make it more saturated with color in the middle.

7 Click as shown

A new gradient color swatch appears.

   Apply the indicated values

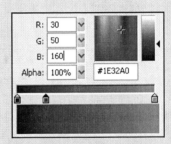

8 Zoom in on the button to 400%

You'll create another gradient to overlay the original gradient so that the button looks like it's made of glass. This new gradient will create the illusion of light reflecting off the button.

9 Select the Selection tool

   Point to either rounded corner, hold (CTRL), and drag the shape upward

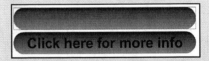

To create a duplicate above the original.

10 In the Color panel, drag the middle color swatch away from the color ramp

To remove the middle gradient color swatch.

   Select the first gradient color swatch, and enter the color values shown

These values create a pure white color for the starting gradient color.

11 Select the ending color gradient swatch

Make this color pure white also

In the R, G, and B boxes, enter 255.

In the Alpha box, enter **0**

Both gradient colors are pure white, but the second one is now transparent. This opaque white to transparent white gradient will create the illusion of light reflecting off the button.

12 In the Tools panel, click

(If necessary) To disable snapping.

Select the Free Transform tool

(In the Tools panel, hold down the mouse button on the Gradient Transform tool and select the Free Transform tool.) You'll resize this gradient oval to fit within the top half of the button.

Resize and reposition the duplicate oval, as shown

Drag the duplicate oval to the top portion of the button. Resize it so that it fits within the top half of the button.

13 Create a duplicate of the selected oval and position it just above the bottom of the button

Select the Selection tool, and hold Ctrl as you drag the oval to the bottom of the button.

14 In the Color panel, from the Type list, select **Solid**

15 Set the color of this oval to white, with an Alpha value of 35%

To complete the illusion of light reflecting off the button, which makes it look like glass.

16 Update the file

Topic B: Soft edges

Explanation

You can create soft edges on objects to allow them to blend more smoothly with the background color of the Stage. To create soft edges, you can either use filters or the Soften Fill Edges command.

Filters

You can use filters to add visual effects such as drop shadows, blurs, glows, and beveled edges to text objects or movie clip or button symbols. You can use filters to create static artistic effects and you can animate filters so that their effects change over time.

Filters work only with Flash Player 8 and newer, which is an important consideration if you think your target audience is unlikely to have one of the newer Flash Player plug-ins.

In order to apply a filter to an object, it must either be a text object, or a movie clip or button symbol.

To convert an object to a symbol:

1   Select the object and choose Modify, Convert to Symbol. This opens the Convert to Symbol dialog box.

2   In the Name box, enter a name for the symbol.

3   Select either Movie Clip or Button for the symbol type and click OK.

To apply a filter to an object:

1   Select the text object, movie clip, or button symbol.

2   In the Property inspector, click the Add Filter button.

3   From the Filter pop-up menu, choose the filter you want to use.

4   In the Property inspector, set the desired values for the filter.

Do it!

B-1:   Applying filters

Here's how	Here's why
1 Save the current file as **My videoadV8**	(In the current unit folder.) This version of the advertisement will require the Flash Player 8 or newer plug-in.
2 Select the bottom transparent oval you created in the previous activity	If necessary.
3 In the Property inspector, activate the Filters tab	The panel controls are inactive because you can apply a filter only to text, a movie clip symbol, or a button symbol.

Remind students that a symbol is a re-useable Flash element that is stored in a file's library and can be re-used as often as needed without significantly adding to the file size.

4 Choose **Modify,** **Convert to Symbol...**	To open the Convert to Symbol dialog box.
In the Name box, enter **Gel glow**	You'll create a gel-like effect for the button.
Select **Movie Clip**	If necessary.
Click **OK**	Now that the selected shape is a movie clip symbol, you can apply filters to it.
5 In the Property inspector, click ⊞	(The Add filter button.) A warning dialog box appears, indicating that filters will not work with Flash Player 6, with which this file was set to be backwards compliant.
Click **Publish Settings**	To open the Publish Settings dialog box.
6 Activate the Flash tab	
From the Version list, select **Flash Player 8** and click **OK**	
7 Click ⊞	To display the Filter menu.
Select **Blur**	To apply the Blur filter.
In the Property inspector, change the Blur X value to **3**	By default, the Lock icon to the right of the Blur X and Blur Y values is selected, so changing the Blur X value also changes Blur Y.
8 Convert the top transparent shape to a movie clip named **Gel highlight**	Select the top transparent shape and choose Modify, Convert to Symbol. In the Convert to Symbol dialog box, enter the name in the Name box, select Movie Clip, and click OK.
9 Add a Blur filter with a value of 1.5 in both the X and Y boxes	
In the Property inspector, from the Quality list, select **High**	To make the blur appear as smooth as possible.
Click outside the Stage	Click here for more info
	To deselect the button.
10 Update and close the file	

The Soften Fill Edges command

Explanation

If you want to soften the edges of an object, but do not want to use a filter because you need to ensure compatibility with Flash Player version 6, you can use the Soften Fill Edges command to create soft edges.

The Soften Fill Edges command creates multiple outlines at a gradually reduced opacity, as demonstrated in Exhibit 4-4. In this example, the object (shown on top) is given different degrees of the Soften Fill Edges command. In the middle example, the effect has 3 "steps"; the number of colors from the fill color to the last transitional color. In the bottom example, the effect has 10 steps, giving the edge a softer appearance. The effect is more evident at a lower magnification.

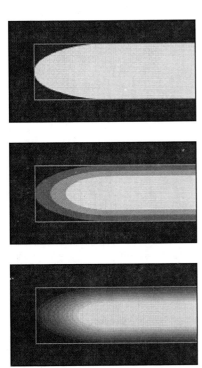

Exhibit 4-4: An object (top) and varying degrees of the Soften Fill Edges command

Do it!

B-2:   Softening fill edges

Point out that the filter method yields smoother, easier-to-edit results, but that this method is compatible with older-version Flash plug-ins.

Here's how	Here's why
1 Open My videoad.fla	(From the current unit folder.) You'll soften the edges of the gel button shapes by using a method compatible with Flash Player 6.
2 Select the first keyframe in the button layer	If necessary.
3 With the Selection tool, click the gel button	
4 Zoom in to 400%	

5	Double-click the right rounded corner of the button	To edit the group.
	Select the bottom transparent shape	
6	Choose **Modify**, **Shape**, **Soften Fill Edges...**	To open the Soften Fill Edges dialog box.
	In the Distance box, enter **8**	
	In the Number of steps box, enter **10**	
7	Select **Inset**	Selecting Inset prevents the shape from enlarging to accommodate the changes.
	Click **OK**	
8	Select the top transparent shape	
9	Open the Soften Fill Edges dialog box	Choose Modify, Shape, Soften Fill Edges.
	Set the Distance value to **8**, the Number of steps value to **10**, and the effect to **Inset**	If necessary.
	Click **OK**	
10	In the Magnification box above the workspace area, enter **2000**	To view the button close up.
	Scroll as necessary to view the left edge of the effect	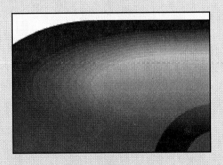
		At high magnification, you can see the steps— the "stacked" colors that create the effect.
11	Update and close the file	

Point out that editing a shape to which Soften Fill Edges is applied involves working with the extra objects individually, which is much more difficult than editing a Blur filter setting.

Unit summary: Formatting objects

Topic A   In this topic, you created **custom colors** and **gradients** and saved them as **swatches** for repeated use. You also learned how to use the Gradient Transform tool, and apply **transparency** to an object.

Topic B   In this topic, you learned how to apply **filters**, and you used the **Soften Fill Edges** command to create an effect that's compatible with older versions of Flash Player.

Independent practice activity

In this activity, you'll create a custom color, use it in a gradient, and create a soft-edged, semi-transparent shadow shape for the buttons.

1 Open quicknavigator.fla from the Practice subfolder in the current unit folder, and save it as **My quicknavigator.fla**.

2 Create a custom color with values of R: 180, G: 60, B: 0, and Alpha: 100%. Add the color to the Swatches panel.

3 Apply the custom color to the buttons and reddish text. (*Hint*: Drag a selection marquee around all of the buttons and text boxes; then select the swatch from the Swatches panel.)

4 Apply a linear gradient to the curved shape on the left of the Stage, with two black color gradients and one with the new color you created, as shown in Exhibit 4-5.

5 Select the Gradient Transform tool and drag the handles so that it runs vertically from the top to the bottom of the shape, as shown in Exhibit 4-6. (*Hint:* Drag the rotation handle down to rotate the selection.)

6 Select the circle to the left of Sauces, and give it a black fill.

7 Convert the circle to a Movie Clip symbol named **Shadow**.

8 In the Property inspector, activate the Filters tab and add a Blur effect, with X and Y values of 8, as shown in Exhibit 4-7.

9 Activate the Properties tab and set the Color value to **Alpha** at 50%, as shown in Exhibit 4-8.

10 Right-click the blurred circle and choose Cut from the shortcut menu. Right-click the circle to the left of Spices and choose Paste. (*Hint:* If the cut circle pastes to a different part of the Stage, move it so that it covers the Spices circle. You might want to turn off snapping or use the arrow keys to position the shadow.)

11 Choose **Modify, Arrange, Send to Back** and position the dot as shown in Exhibit 4-9.

12 Delete the circle to the left of Seasonings.

13 Select the dot and shadow in the Spices layer; then copy and paste them in the Sauces and Seasonings layers, as shown in Exhibit 4-10.

14 Update and close the document.

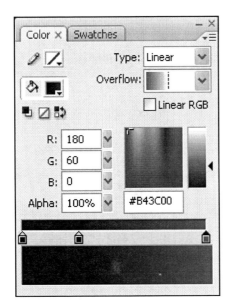

Exhibit 4-5: The Color panel after step 4

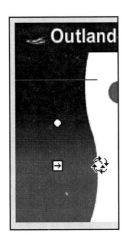

Exhibit 4-6: The Stage as it appears after step 5

Exhibit 4-7: The blurred circle as it appears after step 8

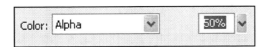

Exhibit 4-8: An Alpha value of 50%, as specified in step 9

Exhibit 4-9: The shadow position after step 11

Exhibit 4-10: The Stage as it appears after step 13

Review questions

1 Which color models can you use to create custom colors? (Choose all that apply.)

   A HSL

   B CMYK

   c RGB

   D HSI

2 You can control the transparency of a color by adjusting its:

   A visibility.

   B see-through property.

   c alpha value.

   D transparency value.

3 How can you save a custom color as a swatch?

   A Double-click the color preview in the Color panel.

   B Choose Add Swatch from the Color panel Options menu.

   C Click Save Color in the Property inspector.

   D Right-click the color preview in the Color panel and choose Save Color.

4 A gradient is:

  A a shape that has a steep incline or decline.

  B a fill that gradually changes from one color or shade to another.

  C a texture that you can apply to a shape.

  D another name for a custom color.

5 How can you remove a color from a gradient?

  A Drag the color swatch away from the color ramp.

  B Right-click the color swatch in the color ramp and choose Remove.

  C Double-click the color swatch in the color ramp.

  D Select the color swatch in the color ramp and press Delete.

6 To soften the edges of an object:

  A you must use a filter.

  B you can use a filter or the Soften Fill Edges command.

  C you must use the Soften Fill Edges command.

  D draw smooth shapes around the edges.

7 Which statements about the Soften Fill Edges command are true? (Choose all that apply.)

  A The Soften Fill Edges command creates multiple outlines at a gradually *increased* opacity.

  B The *fewer* steps you define for the Soften Fill Edges command, the softer the edges appear for the object.

  c The Soften Fill Edges command creates multiple outlines at a gradually *reduced* opacity.

  D The *more* steps you define for the Soften Fill Edges command, the softer the edges appear for the object.

8 To apply a filter to an object:

  A the object must either be a text object or a movie clip or button symbol.

  B the object must either be text or a vector shape.

  C the object must be a symbol.

  D the object must be a raster graphic.

Unit 5

Timeline animation

Unit time: 75 minutes

Complete this unit, and you'll know how to:

A Create a simple frame-by-frame animation.

B Create motion tweened animations.

C Create a looping animation by using a movie clip symbol.

Topic A: Frame-by-frame animation

Explanation

Many Web page designs and advertisements are effective with only static elements, but animations often can more effectively attract a user's attention and interest. You can use Flash to animate objects by using several methods. First, you'll explore simple frame-by-frame animation.

You create a frame-by-frame animation by altering contents slightly on adjacent keyframes in the Timeline, which creates an effect similar to flipbook animation. Frame-by-frame animation can be practical when you need to create a simple animation containing only a few animated steps, or when you are creating a complex animation that involves more than object movement.

Keyframes and animation

To create a frame-by-frame animation, you'll need to create several keyframes, and change the content in each keyframe. When the animation playback hits the keyframes in rapid succession, the result is an illusion of movement, or animation.

Do it!

A-1: Creating frame-by-frame animation

Here's how	Here's why
1 Open animation.fla	From the current unit folder.
Save the file as **My animation.fla**	In the current unit folder.
2 Click frame 10 in the pizzazz layer	
	The text for this layer—"pizzazz"—is selected on the Stage. You'll make this text appear to shake.
Press F6	To add a keyframe. You could also right-click the frame and choose Insert Keyframe.
Add keyframes in the pizzazz layer to frames 11 through 15	
	A change to the content will occur at each keyframe. When the animation is played, these successive changes will create the illusion of motion.

3 Zoom in on the word **pizzazz** to 200%

4 Select keyframe 10 in the pizzazz layer

   Press (→) twice   To move the text box slightly to the right.

5 Select keyframe 12 in the pizzazz layer

   Press (→) twice   To move the text box slightly to the right.

   Select keyframe 14 in the pizzazz layer

   Press (→) twice   To move the text box slightly to the right. These slight moves back and forth will make the text appear to shake.

6 Click frame 1

Tell students that this is just a simple animation that serves as an example of a practical use of frame-by-frame animation.

   Press (↵ ENTER)   To play the application. The word "pizzazz" appears to jitter for a moment, and then stops and remains in position.

Topic B: Motion tweening

Motion tweening is an animation process in which you create keyframes that contain various states of an object (position, size, and so on), and Flash fills in all the intermediate states of the object be*tween* those keyframes.

For example, if you want to create an animation of a logo moving from one side of the Stage to the next, you could accomplish it with only two keyframes—one for the starting position of the logo and another for the ending position. Flash fills in the blanks so that you don't have to create a keyframe for multiple steps. Motion tweens can animate more than the position of an object. You can use motion tweening to animate an object's size, rotation angle, filter settings, and other properties.

If you want to animate an object by using a motion tween, you should put that object on its own layer. To perform a motion tween, an object also must be converted to a symbol.

To create a motion tween for an object:

1   Move the object to its own layer.
2   Convert the object to a symbol.
3   On the layer containing the object, create a starting keyframe.
4   With the starting keyframe selected, set the desired properties for the object to establish its beginning state.
5   On the layer containing the object, set the ending keyframe.
6   With the ending keyframe selected, set the desired properties for the object to establish its end state.
7   Select any frame between the two. Then, in the Property inspector, from the Tween list, select Motion. You can also right-click between the keyframes and choose Create Motion Tween.

Easing

By default, tweened frames play at a constant speed. By setting the Ease value in the Property inspector, you can set an animation to accelerate or decelerate. Positive values start a tween rapidly and decelerate the tween toward the end of the animation. Negative values start the tween slowly and accelerate the tween toward the end of the animation.

Scrubbing

To view a tweened animation in the Timeline without previewing the application, you can *scrub* in the Timeline, which simply means dragging the playhead back and forth through the frames spanning the tween, as shown in Exhibit 5-1.

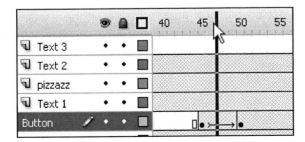

Exhibit 5-1: Dragging the playhead back and forth to view the animation

Do it!

B-1:   Creating a tweened animation

Here's how	Here's why
1 Zoom out to 100%	To view the entire stage. (You might need to scroll to see the entire stage.)
2 With the Selection tool, select the button	
Convert the button to a movie clip symbol named **Click here**	Choose Modify, Convert to Symbol.
3 Add a keyframe at frame 50 on the Button layer	Click frame 50 on the button layer and press F6.
4 Select the keyframe at frame 45 on the Button layer	
Press and hold (SHIFT)	Holding Shift keeps the movement of the drag horizontal.
Drag the button off the stage to the right	
5 Scrub in the Timeline from frame 40 to frame 55, approximately	The button changes position suddenly at frame 50. You'll create a motion tween for the button between frames 45 and 50 so the animation is smoother and the button appears on the Stage gradually.
6 Select the keyframe at frame 45 of the Button layer	
In the Property inspector, from the Tween list, select **Motion**	
	An arrow representing the motion tween appears in the span of frames between the two keyframes.
Scrub in the Timeline again between frames 40 and 55	To view the motion tween. Flash "fills in" the spaces between the two keyframes to complete an animation. Next, you'll make the button appear to grow as it slides onto the Stage.

The playhead must be at the end of the frames.

You're defining it as a movie clip rather than a graphic symbol because you want to further animate the button later.

Tell students to drag the playhead back and forth.

7 Select the keyframe at frame 45 of
   the Button layer

   Select the Free Transform tool

   Drag the right transform handle to
   the left, as shown

To make the button very narrow.

8 Select the Selection tool

   Press and hold (SHIFT)

   Drag the button close to the Stage,
   as shown

*Now you'd like the
button to appear to spring
onto the Stage,
accelerating its motion
toward the end of its
movement. To achieve
this, you need to apply a
negative Ease value.*

9 Drag the playhead to frame 1, and
   press (↵ ENTER)

To play the animation from the beginning. The
button appears to grow as it moves onto the
Stage. The motion tween takes the small starting
state and the complete button in the end state
and fills in all the steps between them.

10 Select frame 45 in the Button
    layer

11 In the Property inspector, drag the
    Ease slider down to –100

To make the animation start slowly and
accelerate near the end.

    Click the Ease box

(If necessary.) To set the value.

*Tell students to play it a
few times if necessary to
notice the effect.*

    Press (↵ ENTER)

To view the Ease effect as the animation plays.
The effect is subtle in this case.

12 Update the file

Animating color effects

Explanation

In the same way that you can use motion tweens to animate the position or transform properties of an object, you can use motion tweens to animate color effects such as alpha value, brightness, or tint.

To animate a color effect:

1 Move the item you want to animate to its own layer.

2 Create a keyframe for the first frame of the animation.

3 Convert the item to a symbol (a movie clip symbol for a static object, as opposed to a button).

4 In the Property inspector, from the Color list, select a color animation type (Brightness, Tint, Alpha, or Advanced).

5 Specify the settings for the option you selected in step 4.

6 Create a keyframe for the last frame of the animation in the same layer.

7 From the Color list, select the same color animation option (if necessary), and settings for that option.

8 In the Timeline, right-click between the two keyframes and choose Create Motion Tween. (You can also use the Property inspector to set the tween.)

B-2: Animating an alpha value

Here's how	Here's why
1 Select the keyframe at frame 25 of the Text 2 layer	To select the text "Buy Cooking with Outlander today!"
On the Stage, right-click the text for this layer, as shown	

ome pizzazz...
Buy
Cooking
with   Cut
Outlan   Copy
Paste
today Copy Motion
Copy Motion as

	To display a shortcut menu.
Choose **Convert to Symbol...**	To open the Convert to Symbol dialog box.
Name the symbol **Cooking MC** and set it as a movie clip	
2 In the Timeline, create a keyframe in frame 30 of the Text 2 layer	
3 Select frame 25 of the Text 2 layer again	The text on this layer is now a symbol, so you can set its alpha value and create a motion tween for it.
On the Stage, click the corresponding text	To make it active.
4 In the Property inspector, from the Color list, select **Alpha**	
Drag the Alpha slider down to 0	At frame 30, the symbol still has its default alpha value of 100, so the tween will create the illusion of the text fading in.
5 Right-click any frame between frames 25 and 30	(In the Text 2 layer.) To display a shortcut menu.
Choose **Create Motion Tween**	
6 Drag the playhead to frame 1, and press ⏎ ENTER	To play the animation from the beginning.
7 Update the file	

Topic C: Movie clip animation

Explanation

If you want an animation to play independently of the main Timeline, you can place the animation in a movie clip symbol. Movie clips have their own timelines, so you can use them to create animations that loop repeatedly even though the main application plays only once. For example, you might want to create a subtle repeating animation for an object, such as a logo, on the Stage.

You can also animate movie clip symbols themselves. For example, say you want to create an animation of a walking stick figure. You can animate the movement of the figure's body within a movie clip symbol because those movements will continuously repeat, and then use a motion tween to animate the movement of the movie clip symbol itself across the Stage.

Movie clip symbol behaviors

Movie clip symbols provide a lot of flexibility when you need to create complex animations. You should keep the following considerations in mind when using movie clip symbols:

- Movie clip symbols have their own timelines. To access the movie clip symbol's timeline, double-click the movie clip symbol in the Library.
- You can place an instance of a movie clip symbol in one frame of the main Timeline and the animation will play in its entirety, even if the main Timeline is stopped.
- Movie clip animation will repeat infinitely even if the main Timeline is stopped.

Accessing a movie clip's timeline

To access a movie clip's timeline, double-click the movie clip symbol in the Library or double-click an instance of the symbol on the Stage.

Do it!

C-1: Creating a looping animation

Here's how	Here's why
1 Double-click the blue button	You'll edit this movie clip.
Observe the top of the workspace area	 You're now editing the movie clip named "Click here." It has its own timeline, independent of the main Timeline.
2 Click frame 20	
Press (F5)	To add frames to the movie clip timeline.

You need to make the button pulse by raising and lowering the button's alpha value over time. By starting and ending at 100%, the pulsing will appear to be continuous.

3	Double-click the button	So that you can edit the button group's objects individually. You'll move the text to a new layer, because you don't want the transparency of the text to change.
	Zoom in on the button to 400%	
	Click inside the capital C, as shown	

		(To select the text.) A selection border should appear around the text, as shown. You'll move this text to a new layer.
	Choose **Edit**, **Cut**	To cut the text off the blue button.
4	Click as shown	
		To return to the movie clip's timeline.
	Create a new layer	Click the Insert Layer button.
	Choose **Edit**, **Paste in Place**	Now you'll make the blue background of the button a movie clip symbol. The button background itself needs to be a symbol so that you can create a tween for it.
5	Select Layer 1	To select the button background.
	Convert the button background to a movie clip symbol named **Gel**	
6	In Layer 1, add a keyframe at frame 10	
	Add another keyframe at frame 20	In Layer 1.
7	Click the keyframe at frame 10	
	Click the left edge of the button, as shown	
		To select the Gel movie clip.

Next, you need to create a motion tween to have the alpha value change gradually between frames 1 and 10, and another between frames 10 and 20.

8 In the Property inspector, from the Color list, select **Alpha**

Set the alpha value to **40**

Scrub in the Timeline

The alpha value is 100% until frame 10, where it lightens to 40% alpha, and returns to 100% at frame 20. You'll create a motion tween to make this effect transition gradually.

9 In Layer 1, click between frame 1 and frame 10

10 Create a motion tween

(In the Property inspector, from the Tween list, select Motion.) You created a motion tween between the two keyframes at frame 1 and frame 10.

11 In Layer 1, click between frame 10 and frame 20

12 Create a motion tween

Now the motion tween changes the alpha from 100% to 40% (in frames 1 through 10), and from 40% to 100% (in frames 10 through 20).

13 View the animation

(You can scrub or move the playback to the beginning and press Enter.) The movie clip animation creates the appearance of a pulsing button.

14 Click **Scene 1**

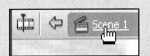

To return to the main Timeline.

Press (↵ ENTER)

To play the animation. The movie clip animation does not appear because only the main Timeline plays when you play an animation this way.

15 Press (CTRL) + (↵ ENTER)

To test the complete application. The movie clip moves onto the Stage and pulses until the application restarts. By default, a movie clip's animation loops when played within the main Timeline.

Close the test window

16 Update and close the file

Unit summary: Timeline animation

Topic A   In this topic, you learned how to create a simple **frame-by-frame animation**.

Topic B   In this topic, you learned about **motion tweening**. You learned that you can create a complete animation with just two keyframes, and allow Flash to "fill in" the steps between them. Then you learned how to make a tweened animation accelerate or decelerate by adjusting the **Ease** value. Finally, you learned how to apply **color effects**.

Topic C   In this topic, you learned how to create a **movie clip animation**. You learned that movie clip animations have their own timelines, and you learned how to navigate between the main Timeline and the movie clip.

Independent practice activity

In this activity, you'll create an animation that makes the background elements fade in and the buttons slide onto the Stage.

1 Open quicknavigator.fla from the Practice subfolder in the current unit folder, and save it as **My quicknavigator.fla**.

2 Click the Background layer to select all of its elements and choose **Modify, Convert to Symbol** to create a movie clip named Background clip.

3 Select the starting keyframe in the Spices layer; then drag it back to frame 1. (You'll re-do the staggered timing for each layer with an animation later.)

4 Reposition the starting keyframes for the Sauces and Seasonings layers in frame 1, as shown in Exhibit 5-2.

5 Create movie clip symbols named **Spices clip**, **Sauces clip**, and **Seasonings clip** from the elements on the Spices, Sauces, and Seasonings layers. (*Hint*: Press F8 to open the Convert to Symbol dialog box.)

6 Deselect the instance by clicking a blank area on the Stage; then select frame 12 in the Background layer in the timeline.

7 Press F6 to add a keyframe, as shown in Exhibit 5-3.

8 Click frame 1 in the Background layer and click the gradient shape to select the symbol.

9 Set the symbol instance on the Stage to 100% Brightness, as shown in Exhibit 5-4.

10 Deselect the instance, select frame 1 in the Timeline, and use the Property inspector to create a Motion tween with an Ease value of –100, as shown in Exhibit 5-5.

11 Play the application to verify that the background elements fade in.

12 Drag the Spices, Sauces, and Seasonings symbol instances to the right of the Stage, as shown Exhibit 5-6. (This will be the starting point of each animation that slides the words on the Stage.)

13 In the Spices layer, add keyframes at frames 9 and 17.

14 With frame 17 selected, drag the Spices instance into position on the Stage, holding Shift as you drag to ensure that it moves horizontally.

15 Select the keyframe at frame 9 and create a motion tween, as shown in Exhibit 5-7.

16 Press Ctrl+Enter to test the application. The background should fade in; then the word Spices should slide onto the Stage from the right. Close the test window after viewing it.

17 In the Sauces layer, add keyframes at frames 12 and 20, move the instance on Stage at frame 20, and create a motion tween at frame 12.

18 In the Seasonings layer, add keyframes at frames 15 and 23, move the instance on Stage at frame 23, and create a motion tween at frame 15, as shown in Exhibit 5-8.

19 Press Ctrl+Enter to test the application. When finished, close the test window.

20 Update and close the file.

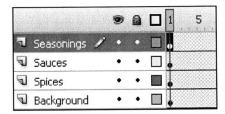

Exhibit 5-2: The starting keyframes as they appear after step 4

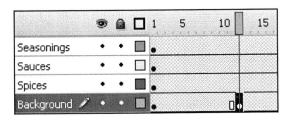

Exhibit 5-3: The timeline as it appears after step 7

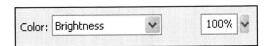

Exhibit 5-4: The brightness value specified in step 9

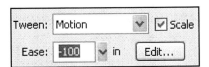

Exhibit 5-5: The motion tween settings specified in step 10

Exhibit 5-6: The positions of the symbol instances at the end of step 12

Exhibit 5-7: The timeline as it appears after step 15

Exhibit 5-8: The timeline as it appears after step 18

Review questions

1 Which type of animation involves creating several keyframes and then changing the content in each keyframe?

  A Motion tweens

  B Stop motion animation

  C Still animation

  D Frame-by-frame animation

2 The most efficient way to create an animation of a shape moving from one side of the Stage to another is to:

  A create a frame-by-frame animation.

  B use a motion tween.

  C create a frame-by-frame tween.

  D create several keyframes and at each keyframe, move the shape in small increments across the Stage.

3 Which statements about motion tweens are true? (Choose all that apply.)

   A You need to move the object you want to animate with a motion tween to its own layer.

   B Motion tweens require three or more keyframes.

   C You need to convert the object you want to animate with a motion tween to a symbol.

   D Motion tweens can animate more than the position of an object.

4 What is the term for dragging the playhead back and forth in the timeline?

   A Sliding

   B Scrubbing

   C Controlled previewing

   D Scene advancing

5 A positive Ease value will:

   A make a tweened animation start slowly and then accelerate toward the end of the animation.

   B make the animation process easier.

   C make a tweened animation start rapidly and then decelerate toward the end of the animation.

   D make a tweened animation gradually gain speed from the start of the animation through to the end.

6 Which are ways to access a movie clip symbol's timeline? (Choose all that apply.)

   A Double-click an instance of the symbol on the Stage.

   B Select the symbol instance on the Stage and click Edit in the Property inspector.

   C Double-click the movie clip symbol in the Library.

   D Select the symbol instance on the Stage and choose View, Timeline.

7 Which statements about movie clip symbols are true? (Choose all that apply.)

   A Movie clip symbols have their own timelines.

   B To access a movie clip symbol's timeline, double-click the movie clip symbol instance on the Stage.

   C Movie clip animation will repeat infinitely even if the main Timeline is stopped.

   D You cannot animate movie clip symbols themselves.

Unit 6

Interactive components

Unit time: 90 minutes

Complete this unit, and you'll know how to:

A Create static buttons, rollover buttons, and invisible buttons.

B Apply basic ActionScript code.

C Apply ActionScript to buttons that control background music in an application.

Topic A: Buttons

Explanation

Buttons allow your Web site users to interact with your Flash applications. For example, you can create rollover effects, or assign a script to a button to control the application timeline, and a variety of other practical and stylistic functions.

Button symbols

To create a button, you need to convert an object to a button symbol. Like the other symbol types, a button symbol has its own timeline. However, the button symbol's timeline is different from the timeline of a graphic symbol or movie clip symbol. The button symbol's timeline, shown in Exhibit 6-1, contains four states: Up, Over, Down, and Hit. These states indicate the condition of the button when a particular action occurs, as described in the following table.

State	Description
Up	Controls the appearance of the button's default state.
Over	Controls the appearance of the button when the user points to the button, but does not click it.
Down	Controls the appearance of the button when it's clicked.
Hit	Defines the region of the button that accepts the mouse click.

As with all timelines, when you want the contents to change from one frame to another, you need to create a keyframe.

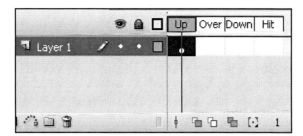

Exhibit 6-1: The timeline for a button symbol

Symbol and instance naming

Every symbol in a file's library, whether it is a button symbol, a movie clip symbol, or a graphic symbol, can be re-used multiple times. Each time you use a symbol on the Stage, you create an *instance* of that symbol.

To make a button do something useful when clicked (other than change appearance), you'll need to create a script that references it by its instance name. Therefore, it's important that you name each button instance on the Stage. This is different than the symbol's name that appears in the Library panel. Each instance of a symbol can have a different name.

To name a symbol instance:

1 Select the symbol instance on the Stage.

2 In the <Instance Name> field in the Property inspector, enter a symbol name, applying best practices, as indicated below.

Instance names can't contain spaces. It's also good programming practice to append an abbreviated suffix to the end of an instance name to denote its type.

- For buttons, append `_btn`

- For movie clips, append `_mc`

Another common programming convention is to begin the name with a lowercase character and capitalize any additional words within. For example, you might name a button `productDetail_btn`. Symbol names can contain spaces. You might consider naming symbols starting with an uppercase letter and including a space to avoid confusion with instance names.

Graphic symbols can't be controlled via ActionScript, and can't be assigned an instance name, so if you want to create interactivity, it's best to define a symbol as either a button or movie clip.

Do it!

A-1: Creating a button symbol

Here's how	Here's why
1 Open soundcontrol.fla	From the current unit folder.
Save the file as **My soundcontrol.fla**	
2 Select the orange square	
Choose **Modify, Convert to Symbol...**	
In the Name box, enter **Stop button**	
Under Type, select **Button** and click **OK**	
3 In the Instance Name box, enter **stop_btn**	
	(In the Property inspector.) It's a good idea to standardize your naming conventions. Start instance names with a lowercase character and end with a suffix denoting its type.
4 Double-click the square	To edit the button in place. The rest of the objects on the Stage dim to indicate that only the button can be edited.
Observe the top of the timeline	This is the button's timeline. It is independent of the main Timeline.

Symbol names can contain spaces, but instances cannot.

5	Click the Over frame, as shown	
	Press (F6)	To add a keyframe.
	Add a keyframe to the Down frame	Click the Down frame and press F6.
6	Click the Over frame	You'll make the button change in appearance when the user points to it. This is called a "rollover."
	Click the orange square again	(If necessary.) To select it.
	Set the Fill color to: Red: **255**, Green: **0**, Blue: **0**	In the Property inspector.
7	Click the Down frame	
	Click the orange square again	(If necessary.) To select it.
	Apply a black fill	On the Property inspector, click the Fill color box and in the color palette, click the black swatch.
8	Go back to the main Timeline	Click Scene 1 at the top of the workspace area.
	Press (CTRL) + (↵ ENTER)	To preview the application.
	Point to the button	The button changes from orange, its default Up state, to red, the Over state.
	Click and hold the button	The button changes from red to black, which is its Down state.
9	Close the test window	
	View the Stop button's timeline again	Double-click the square button to edit it in place.
10	Click the Over frame	
	Below the square, insert the word **STOP**	Use the Text tool.
	Format the text as Arial, 10 points, bold, and dark gray	

Tell them they can also click the red color in the leftmost column in the Fill color palette.

You decide you want the word STOP to appear when the user points to the button.

11 Move the word below the square

(Use the Selection tool.) Place the text box at the bottom of the rectangle so that the user's pointer won't overlap the text.

Copy the selected text block

You need a similar label below the PLAY button you're about to create.

View the main Timeline

12 Convert the triangle into a button symbol named **Play button**

Name the button instance **play_btn**

In the Property inspector, in the Instance Name box.

If the Library isn't visible, tell students to press Ctrl+L. Be sure students click the icon and not the text.

In the Library, double-click the icon next to **Play button**, as shown.

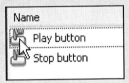

To edit the Play button symbol.

13 Create keyframes in the Over and Down frames of the Play button timeline

In the Over frame, make the triangle red

Click the Over frame, click the triangle, and then, in the Property inspector, apply a red fill color.

14 Choose **Edit**, **Paste in Place**

To paste the text below the triangle. The Paste in Place command used the same relative position of the text to the object above.

Edit the text to read **PLAY**

Use the Text tool.

Tell students to switch to the Selection tool.

15 In the Down frame, make the triangle black

16 Preview both buttons

Press Ctrl+Enter.

Tell students to close the test window.

Return to the main Timeline

Click Scene 1.

Tell students to leave the file open. They'll return to it later.

17 Update the file

Animated buttons

Explanation

Although each button state can have static content, you can add visual appeal and enhanced functionality to a button by animating a button state. For example, you can have the button pulse when the user points to it to provide visual feedback.

To add animation to a button state, insert a movie clip in that state's frame, in the button's timeline. For example, if you want a button to pulse repeatedly only when the user points to the button, you would insert a movie clip containing the pulsing animation in the Over frame of the button's timeline.

Swapping symbols

You might want to change one symbol for another in the same position on the Stage. For example, you might want to replace a static image with an animated movie clip. You can manually remove a symbol instance and place another in the same location, but it's easier to simply swap an instance of one symbol with another.

To swap a symbol:

1   Select the symbol you want to swap.

2   In the Property inspector, click Swap. You can also choose Modify, Symbol, Swap Symbol.

3   In the dialog box, select the symbol you want to swap with the current symbol and click OK.

4   In the Property inspector, name the instance of the swapped symbol.

Do it!

A-2:   Adding a movie clip to a button state

Here's how	Here's why
1 Open pulsebutton.fla	From the current unit folder.
Save the file as **My pulsebutton.fla**	(In the current unit folder.) You'll make a button that pulses when a user points to it.
2 In the Library, click **Pulse mc**	To select it.
In the Library, click the Play button, as shown	
	To preview the movie clip.
In the Library, select **Static mc**	The Play button doesn't appear because this is a static image, so there's nothing to play.
3 On the Stage, click the right edge of the button	Use the Selection tool.

Tell students to verify that a selection box surrounds the entire button.

Tell students that this selects all elements on the Stage.

TIPS
They can also press F8 to open the Convert to Symbol dialog box.

4 In the Property inspector, observe the symbol information	The selected button is an instance of the movie clip Static mc. You'll select the button and the button text, converting the selected elements to a button symbol.
5 Press ⌐CTRL⌐ + ⌐A⌐	To select the button and the button text.
Convert these elements to a button symbol named **Gel button**	Right-click the button, select Convert to Symbol, name it Gel button, select Button, and click OK.
Name the instance of the symbol **gel_btn**	In the Property inspector.
6 On the Stage, double-click the button instance	To edit the symbol in place. Even though the button and text you selected were on separate layers, when you convert them to a symbol, the elements are placed on a single layer within the symbol's timeline.
7 Add a keyframe to the Over frame	
Add a frame (not a keyframe) to the Down frame	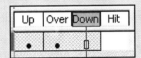
	(Select the Down frame and press F5.) To make the Over and Down states identical.
8 Click an empty area of the Stage	To deselect all items.
Click the outside edge of the button	To select the instance of the Static movie clip.
9 In the Property inspector, click **Swap**	To open the Swap Symbol dialog box.
Select **Pulse mc** and click **OK**	To swap the static button with the pulsing button in the Over and Down states.
10 Rename the instance **gelPulse_mc**	Renaming the instance isn't strictly necessary, because you probably won't write a script to refer to this movie clip. (You'll write one to control the button.)
11 Update the file	
12 Test the application	(Press Ctrl+Enter.) It pulses when you point to it, and continues to pulse when you click and hold the button. It stops pulsing when you move the pointer off the button.
Close the test window	
13 Update and close the file	

Invisible buttons

If you want an entire application to be a clickable region, you need to create an invisible button that is the same size as the Stage. Think of it as a transparent overlay that covers the application—you can see through to the application below, but it serves as a functional layer.

If you are creating a Flash advertisement, you can create a Stage-sized invisible button. Even if you include a visible button on the Stage to entice the user to click, making the entire ad clickable makes it more likely that the viewer will successfully click the ad.

The Hit state

The contents of the Hit frame of a button symbol's timeline determine the interactive area of the button. A Hit frame's contents should generally consist of objects that use a solid fill (the color doesn't matter) with no stroke.

You don't have to place contents in the Hit frame specifically, but if you don't, like in any timeline, the contents will transfer from the right-most defined frame in the timeline. Therefore, if your button contains empty areas, such as buttons made from only text, you'll want to create a solid bounding shape in the Hit frame, to ensure that the holes in the text are clickable regions of the button.

Invisible buttons

You'll likely want to create interactive areas in your applications without having to include a visible button on the Stage. To do this, you can create an invisible button. An invisible button contains objects only in the Hit frame, with the other frames of the button timeline remaining empty.

A-3:   Creating an invisible button

Here's how	Here's why
1 Open interaction.fla	From the current unit folder.
Save the file as **My interaction.fla**	
2 Create a new layer at the top of the layer order	
Name the layer **Invisible button**	It can be helpful to give items obvious names, so that you always know their purpose or function when you work on them at a later date.
3 With the Invisible button layer active, choose **Insert**, **New Symbol...**	To open the Create New Symbol dialog box.
Name the symbol **Invisible button**, set it as a button symbol, and click **OK**	Because you didn't convert an existing object to a symbol, you are now in symbol editing mode and must wait to name the instance.

4 Create a keyframe in the Hit
   frame

Tell students the size
doesn't matter at this
point.

   Draw a red rectangle

(Use the Rectangle tool.) You can use any solid color for the rectangle. Contents of the Hit frame are invisible, but the contents define what area of the button is active.

If it appears locked, tell
students to click it once to
unlock it.

5 In the lower-left corner of the
   Property inspector, verify that [🔒]
   appears

(The unlocked padlock icon.) If a locked padlock appears instead, click it. This will allow you to change the Width and Height values independently from one another.

   Set the width of the rectangle to
   300 and the height to **250**

(In the Property inspector.) To match the Stage size.

   In the X and Y boxes, enter **0**

To align the top-left corner of the rectangle with the top-left corner of the Stage.

6 Switch to Scene 1

Tell students that they are
disabling this option,
which is active by default.

   Choose **Control**,
   Enable Simple Buttons

To clear the option. With this option selected, the button would be invisible to you as you are working.

7 Drag an instance of the Invisible
   button from the Library to the
   Stage

The button appears as a semitransparent blue region, which is Flash's way of indicating that it has only a Hit state—it's designed to define a clickable region, and not meant to be viewed in the final product.

   Set its X and Y values to **0**

To fully and precisely cover the Stage.

This is important, because
a script will refer to this
instance.

   Name the instance
   invisible_btn

8 Update the file

Topic B: ActionScript fundamentals

Explanation

ActionScript is the native scripting language of Flash. You don't have to know how to write ActionScripts to use Flash, but you should be able to write basic ActionScripts if you want to provide user interactivity with objects such as buttons and movie clips.

Why use scripting?

With scripting, you can achieve a greater level of interactivity and functionality, allowing for a wide variety of outcomes based on user actions. Scripting also allows you to create a variety of complex applications, such as interactive games, training aids, and online forms.

However, even simple applications that you might use for Web advertisements or similar projects will require scripting to control basic actions, such as stopping an animation from looping, or enabling a button to take the user to an external Web page.

Behaviors

As an alternative to writing scripts, you can apply Behaviors, which are pre-written blocks of code. They are helpful for novice Flash users because they help users build common interactive functionality into their projects without requiring much experience with ActionScript.

Using behaviors also has its limitations. Because they are added directly to objects, the scripting is scattered throughout the project rather than stored in a centralized location. It can be difficult to see how various pieces of the code are interacting, which can make it difficult for other developers who might need to work on the file. Behaviors might also conflict with other scripts introduced by other developers who work on the file.

Therefore, while behaviors are effective and helpful, particularly for developers who lack scripting experience, it's still best to learn ActionScript if your goal is to become proficient with Flash.

Placing scripts

Although you must attach most behaviors to objects, you can also choose to select an object and add a script by typing the code in the Actions panel, effectively attaching it to the object. But this can make it difficult for you or other developers to locate the scripts.

Instead, it's a good idea to attach scripts to a frame in the application (usually the first frame) or in an external file that is referenced within a script, within the Flash application. This places all relevant code in a central location, which makes it easier to modify and debug.

Many programmers place frame scripts in a layer named Actions at the top of the layer order. This layer contains only actions, and is meant to keep the scripting separate from the application's contents on the Stage.

ActionScript 3.0

Flash CS3 and Flash Player 9 support the newer ActionScript 3.0, and they continue to support ActionScript 2.0. Earlier versions of Flash and Flash Player do not support ActionScript 3.0. ActionScript 3.0 was designed to improve both runtime performance and developer productivity. This course will focus on ActionScript 2.0.

Do it!

B-1: Discussing ActionScript

Question	Answer
1 Describe some advantages to using ActionScript in your Flash applications	*Answers may vary.* • *You can achieve a greater level of interactivity and functionality, allowing for a wide variety of outcomes based on user actions.* • *Scripting also allows you to create a variety of complex applications, such as interactive games, training aids, and online forms.*
2 Describe an advantage to using behaviors	*Behaviors are prewritten code snippets, so they can be helpful to novice Flash users who want to add interactive functionality into their Flash projects without having to learn ActionScript.*
3 Describe a disadvantage to using behaviors	*Behaviors can be difficult to troubleshoot because the code isn't in a single place in the application. They can also conflict with other code in your application that might be introduced by other developers.*
4 Where should you place scripts?	*On a separate layer in the main Timeline or in an external ActionScript file.*
5 Which Flash Player version supports ActionScript 3.0?	*Flash Player 9.*

ActionScript syntax

When creating scripts, there are certain rules that must be followed in order for the script to work properly. In this section, you'll learn basic ActionScript syntax and work with a simple script.

Ending lines

Lines of code must end with either a semi-colon (;) for a standalone line of code or an open bracket ({) for multiple lines of code, as shown in Exhibit 6-2.

```
1  my_sound = new Sound();
2  my_sound.attachSound("bkgdmusic");
3  play();
4  play_btn.onRelease = function(){
5      my_sound.start(0,1000);
6      play_btn._visible = false;
7  }
8  stop_btn.onRelease = function(){
9      my_sound.stop();
10     play_btn._visible = true;
11 }
```

Exhibit 6-2: Lines of ActionScript must end either with a semi-colon or an open bracket

Components of basic ActionScript

When using ActionScript to control objects, you typically create a function, which is a series of steps that should happen when a particular event occurs. As shown in Exhibit 6-3, the syntax for an object command is:

```
objectName.eventName
```

```
invisible_btn.onRelease = function () {
    getURL("site/videos.html")
}
```

Exhibit 6-3: The syntax of a function that controls an object

The object name (in this case, the instance name) is followed by a period, and then the *event handler*, such as onRollOver or onRelease. An *event* is something that occurs, when a user points to an object (onRollOver) or clicks an object (onRelease).

This code is then followed by an equal sign, and then the word function and a pair of empty parentheses, and finally, the function that you assign to respond to the event, enclosed in brackets. For example:

```
my_btn.onRollOver = function() {
        <code that responds to event>
    }
```

A *function* is simply a block of code that executes as a unit. The opening and closing brackets designate the beginning and ending of the function.

Script assistance

Flash helps you write ActionScript code in many ways. First, you can click the plus sign button to add a new item to the code, which pulls up a list of categorized commands. Choosing a command adds that command to the script.

In addition, code hints appear automatically as you type, as shown in Exhibit 6-4, which allows you to select common choices from a list. This occurs when you've defined object types or when you use suffixes such as _btn or _mc to designate that the object in reference is a specific type.

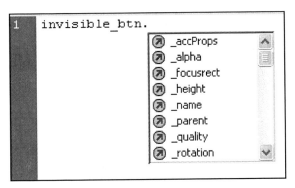

Exhibit 6-4: Code hints appear as you write scripts

Do it!

B-2: Applying basic ActionScript commands

Here's how	Here's why
1 Press (CTRL) + (↵ ENTER)	To test the application in its current state. By default, the application automatically loops when it reaches the end. You'll add a simple ActionScript command to stop the loop after it runs once.
Close the test window	
2 At the top of the layer list, insert a new layer named **actions**	You'll add a stop action to the final frame of the application. To have the action trigger on the final frame, you need to add a keyframe to the final frame.
Add a keyframe to the last frame of the actions layer	On frame 75.
3 Display the Actions panel	(Choose Window, Actions.) You add scripts to your Flash applications in the Actions panel.
In the Commands list, click Global Functions	ActionScript 1.0 & 2.0 Global Functions Movie Clip Control Timeline Control Browser/Network Printing Functions Miscellaneous Functions Mathematical Functions Conversion Functions ActionScript 2.0 Classes
	To expand the category.
4 Expand the Timeline Control category	
Double-click **stop**	To add the `stop();` command to the keyframe at frame 75. (You could also type the command manually.)
5 Test the application	(Press Ctrl+Enter.) The application no longer loops, but the button continues to pulse. This is because the pulsing button is a movie clip, so it has its own timeline and loops independently of the main Timeline.
Close the test window	

Tell students to verify that the keyframe on frame 75 of the actions layer is selected.

If necessary, tell students to resize or reposition the Actions panel.	6 Select frame 1 in the actions layer	You'll add a script to this frame that allows the user to jump to a Web page by clicking anywhere on the ad.
	Click in the code area of the Actions panel	The number 1 appears on the left side, indicating the first line of code. Code numbers can help you to locate and reference lines of code in the development and editing phases of your project.
Tell students that typing the period is what prompts Flash to display the list of code hints.	7 Type `invisible_btn.`	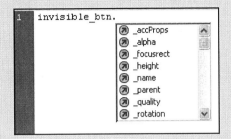
		(Include the period.) To specify the symbol instance that will trigger a response. A list of code hints appears.
Tell students they could also just type it themselves, and that they'll likely develop their own coding preferences.	In the list, double-click **onRelease**	(Scroll down.) To add it to the code.
	8 Press (SPACEBAR) and type `= function()`	Now you'll add the brackets to enclose the function.
	9 Press (SPACEBAR)	
	Type `{`	The bracket, not the parenthesis.
	10 Press (↵ ENTER) twice	
| *It's helpful to create the closing bracket for a block of code as soon as you open one, to avoid a syntax error if you forget to close it later.* | Type `}` | ```
1  invisible_btn.onRelease = function() {
2
3  }
``` |
	11 Click in line 2	Notice that Flash automatically indents code within a code block beginning with an opening bracket. This is a common programming practice to ensure that code is easy to read and items are easy to locate.
	Click 🔁	To display a list of commands.
	From the list, select **Global Functions, Browser/Network, getURL**	
```

| | 12 Observe the code hint | ```
1  invisible_btn.onRelease = function() {
2      getURL();
3              getURL( url, window, method );
4  }
``` |

Flash provides an additional syntax tip that lists the variables that are required with this function.

| Inside the parentheses, type `"site/videos.html"` | ```
1  invisible_btn.onRelease = function() {
2      getURL("site/videos.html");
3
4  }
``` |

Clicking the invisible button will open the file *videos.html*, which is in the folder named *site*.

13 Press F12

To test the application using Publish Preview. The ad appears in a browser window.

  Click anywhere on the ad

To test the invisible button. The videos_html page opens.

14 Close the browser

  Return to Flash

15 Update and close the file

Topic C: Scripting sound control

Explanation

You can use ActionScript to control sounds in an application, allowing you to add background sound that the user can turn on or off, or other sounds that play in response to user-triggered events.

Adding sounds to an application

You can import sounds directly to the Timeline, but it is typically better to control them via ActionScript. When you add a sound directly on the Timeline, you need to have enough frames in the Timeline to play the sound completely. If you control the sound via ActionScript, it is not subject to the amount of frames in the Timeline.

To control a sound via ActionScript, you need to import it as a symbol, and then assign it an identifier. When you create the ActionScript code, you'll type the identifier name to specify which sound in the library to play.

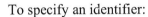

To specify an identifier:

1 Double-click the speaker icon for a sound in the Library panel.
2 Click Advanced.
3 Check Export for ActionScript.
4 Enter a name in the Identifier field.
5 Click OK.

Do it!

C-1: Adding audio with ActionScript

If students closed this file, tell them to open it again.

Here's how	Here's why
1 Activate Mysoundcontrol.fla	If necessary.
2 Choose **File, Import, Import to Library...**	To open the Import to Library dialog box.
Navigate to the current unit folder	
Select **background.mp3** and click **Open**	The sound file is imported to the Library, but not to the Stage.
3 In the Library, double-click the speaker icon to the left of background.mp3	To open the Sound Properties dialog box.
Click **Advanced**	To view additional settings.
Under Linkage, check **Export for ActionScript**	
4 In the Identifier box, type **backgroundMusic**	
5 Click **OK**	

Providing audio controls

Explanation

If you add sound to an application and it plays automatically without requiring user interaction, you should also provide users with controls to turn the sound off.

Dissecting the commands

ActionScript is an *object-oriented language*, meaning that each object is capable of receiving messages, processing information, and sending messages to other objects.

Symbol instances are automatically defined as objects, and you refer to them in ActionScript by their instance names. If you want to control something like a sound, you need to define it as an object so that you can control it with ActionScript.

The following table lists the commands that will be part of a script to control the sound by using buttons.

Command	Description
my_sound = new Sound();	Assigns a new Sound object to the variable "my_sound"
my_sound.attachSound ("backgroundMusic");	Affiliates the "backgroundMusic" identifier with the variable "my_sound"
play();	Enables ActionScript to control the sound (but doesn't actually begin playback)
play_btn.onRelease = function(){	When the user clicks the "play_btn" instance, the function specified after the open bracket will run
my_sound.start(0, 100);	Starts "my_sound" playing at the beginning of the sound, and loops 100 times
stop_btn.onRelease = function(){	When the user clicks the "stop_btn" instance, the function specified after the open bracket will run
my_sound.stop();	Stops "my_sound"

Do it!

C-2: Controlling audio with ActionScript

Here's how	Here's why
1 Add a new layer at the top of the layer list named **actions**	You'll control the buttons by using ActionScript, but instead of attaching code to the buttons directly, you'll reference them within a script attached to the first frame.
2 Select frame 1 in the actions layer	

Be sure that students enter the code in the code window of the Actions panel. They may have to undock the panel or resize it.

3 Enter the following code in frame 1 of the actions layer

```
my_sound = new Sound();
my_sound.attachSound("backgroundMusic");
play();
```

> This code doesn't actually play the sound, but allows it to be controlled by ActionScript.

4 Press (⏎ ENTER) twice	Next, you'll add an onRelease function to the play_btn instance that commands the sound to play when the user clicks the Play button.

5 Enter the following code:

```
play_btn.onRelease = function(){
my_sound.start(0,100);
}
```

> This code tells the sound to play beginning at the first sound sample, and loop 100 times. You'll add an onRelease function to the stop_btn instance that will command the sound to stop when the user clicks the Stop button.

6 Press (⏎ ENTER) twice

7 Enter the following code:

```
stop_btn.onRelease = function(){
my_sound.stop();
}
```

8 Press (CTRL) + (⏎ ENTER)	To test the two buttons.
Click the Play button	To play the background music.
Click the **Stop** button	To stop the music.
Close the test window	

You decide you want to make the Play button invisible after the user has clicked it.

9 In the code window, add the code
   shown in bold below:

⚠ *Make sure students enter the underscore character prior to the word "visible"; the script won't work without it.*

```
play_btn.onRelease = function(){
my_sound.start(0,100);
play_btn._visible = false;
}

stop_btn.onRelease = function(){
my_sound.stop();
play_btn._visible = true;
}
```

	To control the visibility of the buttons.
10 Test the application	After clicking the Play button, it disappears. When you click the Stop button, the Play button reappears.
Close the test window	
Minimize the Actions panel	Now you'll overlap the Stop and Play buttons, so that when users click the Play button, the Stop button appears, and when they click the Stop button, the Play button appears.
11 On the Stage, drag the Stop button on top of the Play button	(Use the Selection tool.) The buttons are the same color, so you can't see the Play button, and the Stop button currently shows as well. You'll add a square that matches the background color, placing it behind the Play button.
12 In the Library, double-click the Play Button icon	To edit the button symbol.
In the button's timeline, add a new layer below the existing one	
Name the layer **background**	
Insert a frame (not a keyframe) in the Down state of the background layer	(If necessary.) To create content for the Up, Over, and Down states.

13 In the background layer, select the
Up frame

Create a square with a solid fill
and no stroke, as shown

In the Property inspector, click the
Fill color box

*Be sure students click one
of the peach-colored
squares and not one of
the gray gridlines.*

Click the background on the Stage

(To sample the background color and fill the
square with that color.) The square's color
matches the background color and it will cover
the Stop button when the Play button is visible.

14 Return to Scene 1

Test the application

When you click the Play button, it appears to
turn into a Stop button. When you stop the
sound, the Stop button appears to turn into the
Play button.

15 Close the test window

Update and close the file

Unit summary: Interactive components

Topic A In this topic, you learned about **button symbols** and button **states**. You learned how to create **static buttons, rollover buttons,** and **invisible buttons.**

Topic B In this topic, you learned some **ActionScript** basics. You learned some **advantages** to using scripts, and you learned basic **ActionScript syntax.** Finally, you applied simple ActionScript commands to stop an application from looping and provide basic interactivity with an invisible button.

Topic C In this topic, you applied ActionScript to existing buttons so that a user can control **background music** in an application.

Independent practice activity

In this activity, you'll make the application stop after playing once, rather than looping continuously. You'll also make the circles to the left of the word "Spices" appear to press down when they're clicked, and you'll make the words and buttons display Web pages when clicked.

1 Open quicknavigator.fla from the Practice subfolder in the current unit folder. Save the file as **My quicknavigator.fla.**

2 Add a layer named **actions.** Create a keyframe on frame 40 in this layer.

3 Activate the Actions panel. In frame 40 of the actions layer, type stop();

4 Press Ctrl+Enter to test the application to verify that it plays only once and then close the test window.

5 If necessary, close or dock the Actions panel so that you can more easily view the Stage.

6 In the Library panel, double-click the icon to the left of **Spices MC** to edit it.

7 Select the circle and its shadow. (Make sure the "Spices" text block is not selected.)

8 Press F8 to convert the selection to a symbol, and create a Button symbol named **Circle btn.** (*Hint*: Verify that Button is selected in the dialog box.)

9 Double-click the button on the Stage to edit it. (Use the Selection tool.)

10 Click the Over frame and press F5 to add a new frame. (This frame is not a keyframe, so the Over state will appear the same as the Up state.)

11 Insert a keyframe in the Down state.

12 Deselect the shapes, and click the circle to select only the top shape. Press the down and right arrow keys twice each. This moves the button over the shadow, which will make it appear pressed down when clicked.

13 Double-click **Sauces MC** in the Library to edit it. The version of the circle here is not the clickable button you just created.

14 Delete the red circle and shadow and drag **Circle btn** from the Library panel to replace them.

15 Delete the circle and shadow from the Seasonings MC symbol, replacing them with Circle btn.

16 Click **Scene 1** above the workspace area to return to the main application.

17 Press Ctrl+Enter to test the application. Click each button to verify that they all appear to push down when clicked, and then close the test window.

18 In the Timeline, move the playhead to the first frame, if necessary.

19 Click the Spices symbol instance to the right of the Stage, and in the Property inspector, enter **spices_mc** in the Instance name box.

20 Name the other instances **sauces_mc** and **seasonings_mc**.

21 Select frame 1 in the actions layer.

22 Open the Actions panel.

23 Enter the following code:

```
spices_mc.onRelease = function() {
     getURL("spices.html", "_parent");
}
```

24 Copy and paste the code twice, and edit the instance name, changing the word **spices** to **sauces** in both places in the second copy, and to **seasonings** in the third copy. Compare your code to Exhibit 6-5.

25 Press F12 to preview the application in a browser. Click each link to open the appropriate page, clicking the Back button to return to the Flash application each time.

26 Close the browser and update and close the file.

```
1   spices_mc.onRelease = function() {
2        getURL("spices.html", "_parent");
3   }
4
5   sauces_mc.onRelease = function() {
6        getURL("sauces.html", "_parent");
7   }
8
9   seasonings_mc.onRelease = function() {
10       getURL("seasonings.html", "_parent");
11  }
```

Exhibit 6-5: The code after step 24

Review questions

1 Which statements are true in regards to naming symbol instances? (Choose all that apply.)

   A You cannot use spaces in an instance name.

   B You should append an abbreviated suffix to the end of the instance name to denote its type.

   C You cannot use uppercase characters in an instance name.

   D You should use at least one numeral in the name to help differentiate it from other symbols.

2 How can you name a symbol instance?

   A Double-click the instance, enter the name, and click OK.

   B Select the instance and enter the name in the Property inspector.

   C Right-click the instance, choose Edit, enter the name, and click OK.

   D Select the instance and choose Modify, Symbol. Enter the name and click OK.

3 Which of the following button symbol states controls the appearance of the button's default state?

   A The Up state

   B The Over state

   C The Down state

   D The Hit state

4 Which of the following button symbol states controls the appearance of the button when the user points to the button, but does not click it?

   A The Up state

   B The Over state

   C The Down state

   D The Hit state

5 Which of the following button symbol states controls the appearance of the button when it is clicked?

   A The Up state

   B The Over state

   c The Down state

   D The Hit state

6 How can you swap a selected symbol instance? (Choose all that apply.)

A Choose Modify, Symbol, Swap Symbol. Select the symbol you want to swap with and click OK.

B Double-click the symbol instance. Select the symbol you want to swap with and click OK.

C In the Library panel, click New Symbol. Select the symbol you want to swap with and click OK.

D In the Property inspector, click Swap. Select the symbol you want to swap with and click OK.

7 How can you create an invisible button?

A Place objects only in the Up frame.

B Place objects only in the Hit frame.

C Place objects only in the Over frame.

D Place objects only in the Down frame.

8 Which statements about ActionScript are true? (Choose all that apply.)

A The best way to add ActionScript is by selecting an object and typing the code in the Actions panel.

B Many programmers place frame scripts in a layer named Actions at the top of the layer order.

C As an alternative to writing scripts, you can apply Behaviors, which are pre-written blocks of ActionScript.

D With scripting, you can achieve a greater level of interactivity and functionality.

9 Which of the following ActionScript code blocks will successfully open a Web page named about.html when you click a button named MyButton?

A
```
MyButton(onRelease) = {
    GetURL ("about.html")
    }
```

B
```
MyButton.onRelease = {
    GetURL ("about.html")
    }
```

C
```
MyButton.onRelease = function(){
    GetURL (about.html)
    }
```

D
```
MyButton_btn.onRelease = function(){
    GetURL ("about.html")
    }
```

Unit 7

Publishing

Unit time: 40 minutes

Complete this unit, and you'll know how to:

A Create content that's accessible to screen readers.

B Test a Flash application to verify that it loads in a browser within a reasonable timeframe.

C Publish a Flash application as a SWF file and insert it into a Web page.

Topic A: Accessibility

Explanation

Your Flash applications are likely to be viewed by users with alternative browsing devices, such as screen readers, which read aloud the contents of a Web page. By default, static text in Flash applications is accessible to screen readers. However, graphic objects require that you add textual information to them. You can make Flash content more accessible by using the Accessibility panel, shown in Exhibit 7-1.

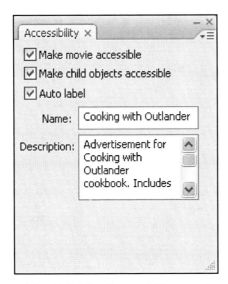

Exhibit 7-1: The Accessibility panel

To add accessibility enhancements to a Flash application:

1 Deselect any objects on the Stage.

2 In the Property inspector, click the Edit accessibility settings button to open the Accessibility panel. You can also choose Window, Other Panels, Accessibility, or press Shift+F11.

3 Verify that the Make movie accessible check box is checked. You can also check the following check boxes, depending on the content you're working with:

- *Make child objects accessible.* If your application includes movie clips, this option enables embedded text objects to be available to the screen reader.

- *Auto label.* This option associates text next to another object, such as an input text field, to be used as a label or title for that object.

4 In the Name box, enter a descriptive name for the application.

5 In the Description box, enter a description of the application.

To make graphic objects in an application accessible:

1 Select a graphic object on the Stage.

2 In the Accessibility panel, in the Name box, enter a name for the graphic.

3 In the Description box, enter a brief description of the graphic. If the name of the graphic is descriptive enough to define what it is, this step might not be necessary.

4 Repeat as necessary for other graphic objects.

Keeping objects from screen readers

When content on a Web page changes, it triggers some screen readers to begin reading the content all over again. With Flash applications, this can be problematic because many applications contain embedded animated objects, which could cause screen readers to restart. To prevent this problem, you can clear the Make Object Accessible check box for certain objects to keep readers from accessing them, or you can clear the Make child objects accessible check box to keep the animation within them from being accessed by the reader. When you do this, you should provide a name and descriptive text for the objects so that users will at least know what the objects are.

Do it!

A-1: Creating accessible Flash content

Here's how	Here's why
1 Open final.fla	From the current unit folder.
Save the file as **My final.fla**	
2 Press (↵ ENTER)	To activate the animation. When the playhead gets to the end of the timeline, all the elements in the animation are visible.
3 In the Property inspector, click ⊠	(The Edit accessibility settings button.) To open the Accessibility panel.
4 Verify that Make movie accessible, Make child objects accessible, and Auto label are checked	Accessibility × ☑ Make movie accessible ☑ Make child objects accessible ☑ Auto label
	You'll add a name and description for the entire ad that screen readers will use to describe it within a page.
5 In the Name box, enter **Cooking with Outlander Ad**	
6 In the Description box, enter **Advertisement for Cooking with Outlander cookbook. Includes animated text, cookbook image, and a navigation link to the OS site.**	You'll also make sure elements within the ad are accessible.
Tell students to move the Accessibility panel, if necessary. 7 Click the text **Give your cooking some pizzazz**	To select it. The Accessibility panel shows that the current selection cannot have accessibility options applied to it. However, because screen readers can access static text, you'll leave it as it is.

8	Click the Outlander DVD image	(The image on the left.) To select it.
	In the Accessibility panel, in the Name box, enter **Outlander Cooking DVD image**	To provide alternate text for the image.
9	Apply alternate text to the Outlander Cooking VHS image	Select the image and enter "Outlander Cooking VHS image" in the Name box in the Accessibility panel.
10	Click the text **Buy Cooking with Outlander today!**	This object is a movie clip instance. Although the instance includes text, it is animated (it fades in), which could cause screen readers to start over each time the animation is triggered. You'll make the object accessible, but you'll adjust it so that screen readers won't have access to the animation.
11	In the Accessibility panel, clear **Make child objects accessible**	Because this also disables screen readers from picking up the text in the object, you'll specify a name for it.
	In the Name box, enter **Buy Cooking with Outlander today**	
12	Select the blue button	The button is also a movie clip instance. Similar to the previous text, the button includes animation (the pulsing effect).
13	In the Accessibility panel, clear **Make child objects accessible**	
	In the Name box, enter **Click here for more info**	
14	Click the text **Available on DVD or VHS**	The text is static (it has no animation), so you'll leave it as is.
15	In the lower-left corner, select the Outlander logo	The logo is also a movie clip instance. However, because there's no animation, there's no potential for screen reader problems.
	In the Accessibility panel, verify that Make child objects accessible is checked	Screen readers will automatically pick up the text in the object, so you don't need to add a name or description.
16	Update the file	

Tab order

Explanation

Most screen readers follow a default order when reading Web content, generally beginning at the top of the page and working down. The same is true of Flash content, unless you specify a reading order by adjusting the tab index. To change the tab index, you need to enter values in the Tab index box, shown at the bottom of Exhibit 7-2. After you've created a custom tab order for objects in a Flash application, you can view the order by choosing View, Show Tab Order.

Exhibit 7-2: The Tab index box in the Accessibility panel

Converting static text to dynamic text

Although static text is available to screen readers, you cannot specify a tab order for static text objects unless they're converted to dynamic text. This is because accessible items require an instance name in order to apply accessibility options to them. To convert static text to dynamic text, select the static text object, and then choose Dynamic text from the Text type list in the Property inspector. Then, enter an instance name in the Instance name box.

Do it!

A-2: Setting the tab index

Here's how	Here's why
1 In the lower-left corner, select the Outlander logo	(If necessary.) You want screen readers to start with the logo text when they begin to read the objects in the animation.
In the Accessibility panel, in the Tab index box, enter **1**	
2 Select the text **Give your cooking some pizzazz**	You want the reader to jump to this text when it finishes with the logo. However, because the text is static, you cannot adjust its tab order.

3 In the Property inspector, from the Text type list, select **Dynamic Text**	The Accessibility panel changes to show accessibility options.
In the Instance name box, enter **text1_txt**	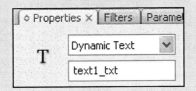
	To create an instance name.
4 In the Accessibility panel, in the Tab index box, enter **2**	
5 Set the DVD and VHS images to be the third and fourth items in the tab order	Select each image, and then enter the values in the Tab index box in the Accessibility panel.
6 Make the text "Buy Cooking with Outlander today!" the fifth item in the tab order	Select the text, and then enter 5 in the Tab index box.
7 Select the text **Available on DVD or VHS**	This is static text.
8 Convert the static text to dynamic text	In the Properties panel, select Dynamic text from the Text type list.
Set the instance name to **text3_txt**	
	In the Instance name box, enter text3_txt
9 Make the text the sixth item in the tab order	
10 Make the blue button the seventh item in the tab order	You'll now view the tab order.
11 Choose **View, Show Tab Order**	Each object in the ad shows a small number next to it, indicating its position in the tab order.
Choose **View, Show Tab Order** again	To hide the tab order.
12 Close the Accessibility panel	
13 Update the file	

Topic B: Testing

Explanation

Before you publish a Flash application, you should optimize it as much as possible and test it. Sometimes you can minimize the size of a Flash application by simplifying the objects in the animation. This in turn could prevent a browser from pausing the animation as it downloads the application.

Optimization

There are many ways you can make the file size of your Flash applications smaller. The following list provides some practical guidelines:

- **Use symbols for objects that appear more than once in the animation.**
- **Group objects whenever possible.**
- **Avoid bitmaps if possible.** If you do need to use bitmaps, include them as stationary objects only. Animated bitmap objects add significantly to the overall file size.
- **Optimize curves whenever possible.** You can sometimes reduce the number of lines used to create a shape by choosing Modify, Shape, Optimize, and then specifying optimization settings in the Optimize Curves dialog box.
- **Use the Web-safe color palette.** Avoid custom colors if possible. Custom colors are stored with the file.
- **Use solid fills rather than gradients, if possible.** Gradients are more complex and make the file size bigger.
- **Reduce the number of fonts and font styles used in the application.**
- **Use shared libraries, if possible.** If you're using some of the same elements in more than one animation, you can put them into a shared library, and users will need to download them only once.
- **Use the MP3 format for sound files.** MP3s tend to provide good quality sound at a small file size.
- **Use tweens instead of frame-by-frame animation.** Frame-by-frame animation tends to create larger file sizes.
- **Place non-animated objects on different layers than animated ones.**

Testing an application

You already know how to preview your animation using the Timeline. However, some interactive functions, such as buttons, don't work directly in Flash. To fully test an application, choose Control, Test Movie (or press Ctrl+Enter). When you do, Flash publishes the movie to a SWF file, and opens the animation in a separate player window. By default, the window begins playing the animation (or interactive content). You can stop the animation by pressing Enter.

You can view additional information about the file by choosing View, Bandwidth Profiler. The profiler, shown in Exhibit 7-3, appears above the application. The left side of the profiler displays information about the application, such as the dimensions, frame rate, and overall file size. The right side shows a bar graph that represents the byte size of each individual frame. To view information about a frame, click it in the graph.

The frame information appears beneath the State category on the left side. The graph also shows a red horizontal bandwidth limit line, which indicates whether a given frame streams in real time with the current modem speed. Frames whose bars rise above the red line can cause loading delays. Typically, the first frame consists of the bulk of the artwork, so that will take longer to download. Often, Flash designers will use preloaders to make the process seem less time consuming. A *preloader* is a quick-loading simple animation that distracts the audience while the first frame loads.

The default Internet connection speed Flash uses to determine download performance is 56K, but you can change the connection speed by choosing View, Download Settings, <connection speed>.

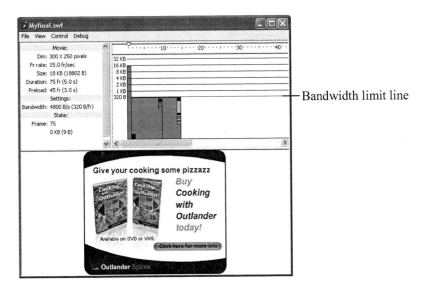

Bandwidth limit line

Exhibit 7-3: The bandwidth profiler

To simulate the amount of time a Flash application will take to download in a typical browser, choose View, Simulate Download. You can correct loading delays by closing the preview window and making the necessary optimization adjustments in Flash.

Do it!

B-1: Testing document download performance

Here's how	Here's why
1 Press `CTRL` + `↵ ENTER`	To open the animation in a separate preview window.
2 Choose **View**, **Bandwidth Profiler**	The bandwidth profiler appears above the animation.
3 Maximize the window	(If necessary.) To view the entire Timeline.
4 Choose **Control**, **Rewind**	To set the animation back to the beginning.
5 Click the first bar in the graph, as shown	
Under State, observe the frame statistics	The first frame is approximately 14KB. The Preload statistic shows that it will take approximately 3 seconds for the animation to load before it begins playing.
6 Choose **View**, **Download Settings**, **DSL (32.6 KB/s)**	The graph contracts horizontally. The Preload time falls to approximately 0.4 seconds.
7 Choose **View**, **Simulate Download**	The Flash application begins to load, just as a browser would need to load it at the current Internet connection speed. It will not appear or begin playing until the first frame is fully loaded.
8 Choose **View**, **Download Settings**, **56k (4.7 KB/s)**	
Choose **View**, **Simulate Download**	Again, the Flash application begins to load similarly to how it would load in a browser. This time, however, the animation loads more slowly because of the slower connection speed.
9 Close the preview window	To return to Flash.

Topic C: Publishing

Explanation

To use a Flash application in a Web page or as a stand-alone application that plays in the Flash Player, you need to publish the Flash file. When you publish a Flash file, it's exported as a SWF file. Browsers that have the Flash plug-in can then open the Flash application.

Publishing options

Most users have browsers that include the Flash Player, which is available for free. You should make sure that your Flash application can play in at least the prior version of Flash Player (and possibly two versions back), especially soon after a new version is released. In this case, because Flash Player 9 is the current version, you should ensure that your projects are also compatible with version 8, or even version 7 for maximum compatibility. You can set the appropriate Flash compatibility in the Publish Settings dialog box.

To set publish options and publish a Flash application:

1   Choose File, Publish Settings to open the Publish Settings dialog box. You can also deselect all objects on the Stage and click the Settings button next to the Publish category in the Property inspector.

2   Activate the Formats tab.

3   Check HTML if you want to create a companion HTML page with the exported SWF file automatically embedded in it.

4   Activate the Flash tab.

5   From the Version list, select the highest Flash Player version for which you want to ensure compatibility.

6   Click Publish. Flash creates a SWF file from the original Flash file. If you checked HTML in step 3, Flash also creates a companion HTML file.

If you want the SWF file to appear within an existing Web page, you need to enter the proper HTML code to embed the file. The easiest way to do this is to copy the code from the companion HTML page that's created when you publish the Flash file and paste it into the desired Web page.

Do it!

C-1: Publishing a SWF file

Here's how	Here's why
1 Choose **File, Publish Settings...**	To open the Publish Settings dialog box.
Activate the Formats tab	If necessary.
Check **HTML**	(If necessary.) To create an HTML file that embeds the SWF file.
2 Activate the Flash tab	
From the Version list, select **Flash Player 7**	To ensure compatibility with browsers that have an older Flash plug-in.
3 Activate the HTML tab	
From the Template list, verify that Flash Only is selected	
4 Click **Publish**	To create the SWF file and companion HTML file.
Click **OK**	To close the Publish Settings dialog box.
5 In Notepad, open My final.html	(From the current unit folder.) In Windows Explorer, right-click My final.html. From the shortcut menu, choose Open With, Notepad.

Point out that an HTML tab appears.

Fewer lines might appear here if Word Wrap is not enabled in Notepad, but this will not affect the activity.

Select the `<object>` tags and the text within them, as shown

```
</script>
<noscript>
        <object classid="clsid:d27cdb6e-ae6
codebase="http://download.macromedia.com/pu
0" width="300" height="250" id="Myfinal" al
        <param name="allowScriptAccess" val
        <param name="allowFullScreen" value
        <param name="movie" value="Myfinal.
/><param name="bgcolor" value="#ffffff" />
bgcolor="#ffffff" width="300" height="250"
allowScriptAccess="sameDomain" allowFullScr
pluginspage="http://www.macromedia.com/go/g
        </object>
</noscript>
</body>
</html>
```

6 Choose **Edit**, **Copy**	
Close Notepad	
7 In Notepad, open clientpage.html	From the current unit folder.

Select the text **Flash_ad_goes_here**

```
<!--AD PLACEHOLDER START-->
Flash_ad_goes_here
<!--AD PLACEHOLDER END-->
</td>
```

Choose **Edit**, **Paste**	To paste the code that embeds the SWF file.
Update and close clientpage.html	

8 In Internet Explorer, open clientpage.html	The Flash file plays in the Web page.
Close Internet Explorer	
9 Return to Flash	
10 Update and close the document	

Unit summary: Publishing

Topic A
In this topic, you learned how to apply **accessibility enhancements** for a Flash application. You learned how to create a general name and description for an application, and apply accessibility settings for objects in the application that screen readers can use to verbally describe the content.

Topic B
In this topic, you learned ways to **optimize** your Flash applications, and you learned how to **test a Flash application** to see how long it takes to download at varying Internet connection speeds. You also learned how to use the **bandwidth profiler** to preview an application.

Topic C
In this topic, you learned how to **publish a Flash application** as a SWF file and insert it into a Web page. You learned that the easiest way to insert it into a Web page is to copy the code from the companion HTML page that Flash creates when you publish the Flash file, and paste it into the HTML code of the desired Web page.

Independent practice activity

In this activity, you'll open a Flash application and apply accessibility options. You'll also preview the application using the bandwidth profiler. Lastly, you'll change publish settings, and publish the file to generate a SWF and a corresponding HTML file.

1. Open quicknavigator.fla (from the Practice subfolder in the current unit folder). Save the file as **My quicknavigator.fla**.

2. Activate the animation so that all the elements are visible.

3. Open the Accessibility panel and add a name and description for the application. (*Hint:* Click the Edit accessibility settings button in the Property inspector to open the Accessibility panel. Enter the name and description in the Name and Description boxes.)

4. Convert the static text "Quick Navigation" to dynamic text. (*Hint:* Select the text and choose **Dynamic text** from the Text type list in the Property inspector. Set the instance name for the text to **quicknav_txt**.

5. Select the Spices button. The button is animated, so manually set accessibility text for it. (*Hint:* In the Accessibility panel, clear Make child objects accessible. Then enter a descriptive name for the button in the Name box.)

6. Set similar accessibility options for the two remaining buttons.

7. Select the curved background shape. Remove any accessibility options for the object. (*Hint:* In the Accessibility panel, clear Make object accessible.)

8. Set the tab order for the application so that screen readers will start with the logo, then go to the "Quick Navigation" text, and then the navigation buttons. (*Hint:* Select each object and enter values in the Tab index box in the Accessibility panel.)

9. Show the tab order. The result should look similar to the example shown in Exhibit 7-4. (*Hint:* Choose View, Show Tab Order.)

10. Preview the application by using the bandwidth profiler. Switch between Internet connection speeds to view the approximate download time. (*Hint:* Press Ctrl+Enter to open the preview window.)

11. Close the preview window and open the Publish Settings dialog box. (*Hint:* Choose File, Publish Settings.)

12 Activate the Flash tab. From the Versions list, select **Flash Player 8**.

13 Click **Publish**, and then click **OK**.

14 Update and close the document.

15 In Internet Explorer, open the My quicknavigator.html file you generated (in the Practice subfolder in the current unit folder).

16 Close all files, and close Adobe Flash CS3 Professional.

Exhibit 7-4: The Flash application after completing step 9

Review questions

1 How can you make a selected graphic object accessible?

   A Double-click the graphic object. Enter a name for the graphic in the Name box. If necessary, enter a description in the Description box and then click OK.

   B Choose Modify, Object. Enter a name for the graphic in the Name box. If necessary, enter a description in the Description box, and then click OK.

   C Enter a name for the graphic in the Name box in the Property inspector. If necessary, enter a description in the Description box.

   D Enter a name for the graphic in the Name box in the Accessibility panel. If necessary, enter a description in the Description box.

2 How can you open the Accessibility panel? (Choose all that apply.)

   A Click the Edit accessibility settings button in the Property inspector.

   B Double-click an object on the Stage.

   C Choose Window, Other Panels, Accessibility.

   D Press Shift+F11.

3 How can you prevent a selected object from being picked up by screen readers?

   A Right-click the object and choose Make object accessible to deselect the option.

   B Clear the Make object accessible check box in the Accessibility panel.

   C Choose Modify, Make object accessible to deselect the option.

   D Double-click the object.

4 How can you convert selected static text to dynamic text?

   A Using the Selection tool, double-click the static text object.

   B Choose Dynamic text from the Text type list in the Property inspector.

   C Right-click the static text object and choose Convert to Dynamic Text.

   D Choose Text, Convert to Dynamic Text.

5 How can you change the tab order for accessible objects?

   A Right-click each object and choose Tab index. In the dialog box, enter a value.

   B Choose View, Show Tab Order. Select each object and enter a value in the Tab index box.

   C In the Property inspector, enter a value in the Tab index box for each object.

   D In the Accessibility panel, enter a value in the Tab index box for each object.

6 True or false? You cannot specify a tab order for static text objects unless they are converted to dynamic text.

   True

7 Which are ways to optimize a Flash file? (Choose all that apply.)

   A Use solid fills rather than gradients, if possible.

   B Use tweens instead of frame-by-frame animation.

   C Use bitmap images as backgrounds whenever possible.

   D Use symbols for objects that appear more than once in the animation.

8 How can you open the Bandwidth Profiler?

   A Press Ctrl+Enter to preview the animation and choose View, Bandwidth Profiler.

   B Choose Window, Bandwidth Profiler.

   C Right-click anywhere on the Stage and choose Open Bandwidth Profiler.

   D Deselect all objects and click Bandwidth Profiler in the Property inspector.

9 Which statements about publishing Flash applications are true? (Choose all that apply.)

   A You should make sure that your published Flash application can play in at least the prior version of Flash Player.

   B During the publishing process, you can specify that Flash creates a companion HTML file.

   C When you publish a Flash application, it's exported as a SWF file.

   D Publishing an application reduces its file size, but you do not have to publish it in order to use it in a Web page.

10 How can you open the Publish Settings dialog box? (Choose all that apply.)

   A Right-click anywhere on the Stage and choose Publish Settings.

   B Choose Window, Other Panels, Publish Settings.

   C Choose File, Publish Settings.

   D Deselect all objects and click the Settings button next to the Publish category in the Property inspector.

Course summary

This summary contains information to help you bring the course to a successful conclusion. Using this information, you will be able to:

A Use the summary text to reinforce what students have learned in class.

B Direct students to the next courses in this series (if any) and to any other resources that might help students continue to learn about Flash CS3.

Topic A: Course summary

At the end of the class, use the following summary text to reinforce what students have learned. It is intended not as a script, but rather as a starting point.

Unit summaries

Unit 1

In this unit, students identified the types of applications they can create in Flash, and students identified the components of the **Flash interface**. They also learned how to use Flash's **Help system**.

Unit 2

In this unit, students learned how to create a new file from a **template**, set **Stage properties**, **import images**, create **text blocks**, apply text **formatting**, draw objects and shapes, and apply **fills** and **strokes**. They also learned how to **transform shapes**, **combine shapes**, and apply **freeform shapes**.

Unit 3

In this unit, students learned how to use **layers** to manage content in a Flash application. They learned how to create, name, and manage layers, and they learned the basics of the **Timeline**. Finally, they learned how to create **frames, keyframes,** and **blank keyframes**, and control the duration of a Flash application.

Unit 4

In this unit, students learned how to create **custom colors** and **gradients** and save them as **swatches** for repeated use. Then they learned how to use the Gradient Transform tool, and apply **transparency** to an object. Finally, students learned how to apply **filters** and the **Soften Fill Edges** command.

Unit 5

In this unit, students learned how to create a simple **frame-by-frame animation**. They learned how to create a **motion tween** animation and accelerate or decelerate an animation. Finally, students learned how to apply **color effects** and how to create a **movie clip animation**.

Unit 6

In this unit, students learned about **button symbols** and button **states**. They learned how to create **static buttons, rollover buttons,** and **invisible buttons**. Then they learned basic **ActionScript syntax** and applied simple ActionScript commands. Finally, students applied ActionScript to existing buttons so that a user can control background music in an application.

Unit 7

In this unit, students learned how to apply **accessibility enhancements** to a Flash application so that users with alternative browsing devices can access the content. They created a **general name** and **description** for an application and they learned how to **set accessibility options** for objects in an application that screen readers can use to verbally describe the content. They also learned how to use **the bandwidth profiler** to preview how long it will take to download an application at varying Internet connection speeds. Lastly, students learned how to **publish a Flash application** as a SWF file and **insert it into a Web page**.

Topic B: Continued learning after class

Point out to your students that it is impossible to learn to use any software effectively in a single day. To get the most out of this class, students should begin working with Flash CS3 to perform real tasks as soon as possible. We also offer resources for continued learning.

Next course in this series

This is the first course in this series. The next course in this series is:

- *Flash CS3: Advanced*

Other resources

For more information, visit www.axzopress.com.

Flash CS3: Basic

Quick reference

Button	Shortcut keys	Function
▶	V	The Selection tool selects or moves an object.
▧	Q	The Free Transform tool transforms images, instances, or text blocks; you can resize, rotate, distort, or envelop images, instances, or text blocks.
▢	R	The Rectangle tool creates rectangles and squares.
T	T	The Text tool inserts a text block.
✎	Y	The Pencil tool draws freeform lines and shapes.
▱	E	The Eraser tool erases unwanted parts of a shape.
🔍	M or Z	The Zoom tool magnifies a particular area of a drawing.
B		Applies bold formatting.
¶		Opens the Format Options dialog box.
≣		Centers text.
◎		Activates or deactivates the Object Drawing model.
🖋	S	The Ink Bottle tool changes the stroke of a shape, or adds a stroke to a shape that originally didn't have one.
🪣	K	The Paint Bucket tool changes the fill color of a shape, or adds a fill to a shape that originally didn't have one.
╲	N	The Line tool draws straight lines.
⌐		Displays a list of the three freeform options: Straighten, Smooth, and Ink.

Button	Shortcut keys	Function
		Turns snapping to objects on or off.
	A	The Subselection tool selects and modifies individual points on a path.
	L	The Lasso tool creates an irregularly shaped selection.
		Creates a new layer.
		Deletes layers.
		Creates a layer folder.

Glossary

ActionScript

The native scripting language of Flash.

Alpha

The amount of opacity or transparency given to a color. A value of 0% is fully transparent, and a value of 100% is fully opaque.

Blank keyframe

A keyframe that does not yet contain any content. A blank keyframe is indicated by a white circle on a frame.

Event

In scripting, an event is something that occurs, such as when a user points to an object (onRollOver) or when the user clicks an object (onRelease).

Fill color

The color inside a shape or object.

Frame rate

The playing speed of an animation. It's measured in frames per second (fps).

Function

In scripting, a block of code that executes as a unit, typically when a particular event occurs.

Gradient

A fill color that gradually changes from one color or shade to another.

HSL color model

A color model that's based on the hue (a particular color within the spectrum), saturation (the intensity of the hue), and luminosity (the amount of light in the color).

Keyframe

Defines the moment in the animation where an action or change of some kind occurs. A keyframe is indicated by a black circle on a frame.

Linear gradient

A gradient that changes color along a single axis.

Motion tweening

An animation process in which you create keyframes that contain various states of an object (position, size, and so on), and Flash fills in all the intermediate states of the object be*tween* those keyframes.

Preloader

A quick-loading simple animation that distracts the audience while the first frame loads.

Radial gradient

A gradient that changes color from a specific point outward.

Raster graphics

Images based on a grid of pixels, such as GIF and JPEG images.

RGB color model

A color model that's based on the intensity of red, green, and blue in the color.

Stage

The Stage is the main work area where you place and view the graphics, video, and other visual elements of the application. The Stage represents a Web browser.

Static image

An image of any type that is not part of an animation or dynamic component.

Stroke color

The outline color of a shape or object.

Symbol

A re-useable Flash element that is stored only once, but can be re-used as often as needed without significantly adding to the file size. There are three types of symbols—graphic, button, and movie clip symbols.

Timeline

The component you use to specify the timing of each element's appearance and animation.

Vector graphics

Images that are defined mathematically, and typically have smaller file sizes than comparable raster graphics.

Index